GREAT CANADIAN BOOKS OF THE CENTURY

GREAT

Vancouver Public Library
foreword by Bill Richardson

CANADIAN

BOOKS OF THE

CENTURY

Douglas & McIntyre
VANCOUVER/TORONTO

Douglas & McIntyre Ltd.
2323 Quebec Street, Suite 201
Vancouver, British Columbia V5T 4S7

Canadian Cataloguing in Publication Data
Main entry under title:
Great Canadian books of the century
Includes index.

ISBN 1–55054–736–4
1. Canadian literature—20th century—Bibliography. 2. Canada—
Civilization—20th century—Bibliography. I. Vancouver Public Library.
Z1365.G73   1999 016.97106   C99-910689-9

Editing by Nancy Pollak, Saeko Usukawa, and Lucy Kenward
Cover and text design by Peter Cocking
Cover photograph by Chick Rice
Printed and bound in Canada by Transcontinental Printing and Graphics, Inc.
Printed on acid-free paper ∞

The publisher gratefully acknowledges the support of the Canada Council for the
Arts and of the British Columbia Ministry of Tourism, Small Business and Culture.
The publisher also acknowledges the financial support of the Government of
Canada through the Book Publishing Industry Development Program.
Canadä

CONTENTS

Foreword

by Bill Richardson

O nce upon a time, I was a librarian. I suppose I still am a
librarian, even though it's not what I call myself if pressed
for a professional descriptor. Somewhere I have a certificate that
swears to my pedigree. I haven't seen it in years, but I seem to
recollect it was an attractive document, articulated with elegant
flights of calligraphy. It was tagged with a jaunty and official
seal, like a big boutonniere, and it was surely suitable for framing.
That it now lies full fathom five in the bottom of some crate,
rather than hanging in a place of proud prominence, is not a measure of anything like disregard for so hard-earned a qualification.
It's simply a symptom of the thoughtlessness that taints my
relationship with all such souvenirs.

I spent the better part of ten years working in public
libraries, and while I have forgotten many of the specifics of my
various engagements, I still remember very clearly the impetus
for my joining the profession in the first place. In the fall of 1977,
as the bewildered possessor of a newly minted B.A., and certain
of nothing beyond the fact that I didn't want to teach, I applied
to and was hired by the City of Winnipeg as a "Public Library
Reference Assistant." Why I was accorded this boon I can't imagine, as I had not one relevant qualification. It may have been

on the strength of my interview outfit: a powder blue, polyester leisure suit complemented by a shirt that owed a huge debt to chemistry. Or it may have been that the committee was astonished into submission because of my gender. Back then, it was novel for men to apply for such a position as Public Library Reference Assistant when they could readily work under the aegis of Parks or Sanitation at something bracing and outdoors and manly.

Anyway, the upshot was that the job was mine, and I loved it. I loved the work itself, which was the challenging business of rooting around in reference sources to find the answers to questions that were puzzling to the tax-paying public. But more than the work, I loved my colleagues, both the other "paraprofessionals" and the accredited librarians. They were funny and smart and well-read and eccentric and radical. They really believed in the democratic ideal of the public library, and it was through talking to them that I understood for the first time something of the vastness of its possibilities, of its importance as a social institution. Those librarians were good people, wholly worthy of emulation, and I wanted to be just like them. Through some primitive process of magic association, I felt I could achieve this simply by aping their academic accomplishments and getting the same credentials as they had earned. And so, off I went to library school.

As it turned out, I was a lousy librarian: disorganized and inefficient, and with no ready grasp of systems. What's more, I was cranky. I grew impatient with the public, whom we were intended to serve. I found it hard to maintain anything like equanimity when trying to decipher yet another half-remembered title, or a garbled author name. One eventful day, I tried to help a woman find a picture of a dragon. She needed it because she was designing a costume for Hallowe'en. Image after image was laid out before her, a splendid diversity of dragons, big and tall, evil and benign, comic and purposeful. None of them would do. None was the right dragon. I understood that she was looking for the illustration that would match in every detail her own private dragon, the dragon of her imaginings, but such a creature was just not to be found. To ask for a picture of a dragon was reasonable enough, but her absolute need for precise external verification of a figure that lived only in her own fantasies seemed so hopeless, so misguided, so impossible, really. She became tense and I grew testy. Something inside me snapped that afternoon. I felt I had reached the end of my usefulness. It was time to hang another shingle.

The dragon incident took place in a branch of the Vancouver Public Library. Many of the librarians with whom I worked, all those years ago, are still tilling the same fields. They were then, and remain today, skilled and dedicated professionals who would never grow mortally discouraged because of a mild contretemps with a dragon hunter. *Great Canadian Books of the Century* is evidence that they are willing to take on the impossible. Finding an adequate dragon is a snap compared to compiling a list of "great books" that any individual or collective will find wholly satisfying. Many such lists have been, or will be, compiled as we approach the end of the century, but very few will be as diverse as *Great Canadian Books of the Century*. It is an unconventional and fascinating collation. The Vancouver Public Library is fortunate in having librarians with a real expertise in such subject areas as Fine Arts, Literature, Science and Technology, Business and Books for Young People. This project is a testament both to that expertise and to the democratic spirit that plainly reigned over its assemblage. It's a safe bet, for instance, that this is the only list of its kind to include *The Paper Bag Princess* by Robert Munsch cheek by jowl with Jane Jacobs's *The Death and Life of Great American Cities*; or in which *The Double Hook* by Sheila Watson (a predictable and welcome inclusion) would be a near neighbour of the RCAF's *5BX Plan for Physical Fitness*. That there are so many worthwhile titles herein with so relatively little to say to one another is a direct consequence, no doubt, of Sociology and Youth and Business and General Reading librarians duking it out over which of their charges would make the final cut of 133. The result is catholic, surprising, eccentric and provocative. For instance, I find myself wondering why *The Edible Woman* and *The Journals of Susanna Moodie* should represent Margaret Atwood rather than *Survival* and *Selected Poems*. Where are Brian Moore, Gail Anderson-Dargatz, Dionne Brand and Shyam Selvadurai? Where are Paul Hiebert and his alter-ego, Sarah Binks? Where is Ronald Wright, whose novel *A Scientific Romance* should, as far as I'm concerned, share with *Fugitive Pieces* the very upper rung of any such ladder as this.

Of course, these are exactly the quibbles that should come to mind. These are exactly the questions and cavils that such an endeavour should properly encourage. How could it be otherwise? As absolute inclusivity is not a real possibility, an inevitable arbitrariness settles in. The real work of such a list is to jar people out of complacency, to make them say, "Hang on a second! What about...?" And the real reason for celebration is not so much the publication of the list itself, as the fact that so many titles and authors could not be numbered on it, for reasons that are as much practical as they are aesthetic. Congratulations to the staff of the Vancouver Public Library on the publication of a book that is both unusual and delightful; and congratulations as well to that same group for working so tirelessly for so many years as advocates of Canadian books. It is a measure of their success that the task represented by *Great Canadian Books of the Century* is, in the end, a worthy and impossible pleasure.

Preface

Few exchanges are so powerful or intimate as that between
a writer and a reader. Books are great for many reasons.
They can inspire, challenge, educate, entertain, influence,
shape perception, expand experience and touch us so deeply
that they become a part of who we are.

Great Canadian Books of the Century is Vancouver Public
Library's selection of outstanding Canadian works published
in the last hundred years. This celebration of Canadian writers
and writing is an attempt to share our knowledge and our
favourites. Like an informed and enthusiastic guide by your
side, *Great Canadian Books* points out the classics, as well as
some hidden treasures.

In 1997, we were intrigued by a small but ambitious volume,
The New York Public Library's Books of the Century, a selection
of international fiction and non-fiction reviewed by staff from
the New York Public Library to commemorate their hundredth
anniversary. Their work inspired us to create a list of great
Canadian books.

Our challenges were many. We wanted to select titles in
various genres and to involve as many Vancouver Public Library
staff as possible. Over seventy librarians and staff members

contributed to the selection and annotation process. So, although this book is officially authored by Vancouver Public Library, it is really a compilation of the expertise and dedication of every person involved.

Naming outstanding works in many areas was easy. As titles began to surface, however, we realized that they were being chosen for different reasons: some for artistic merit, others for contribution to a field of study, others for their cultural influence. We then decided, in a spirit that itself might be called Canadian, to open our selection criteria to embrace a diversity of excellence.

In this list, a book is considered a Canadian work if it was written by a Canadian author, if the author's work was primarily produced in Canada, if the content or subject is primarily Canadian, or if the work has been critical in shaping our society. A book with a regional subject or focus was included if it also had national significance.

A title had to have been published in the twentieth century and in English, or in an English translation. If a book was out of print, it had to be readily available in public libraries. A work of drama had to have been published in book form. An older work selected for historical importance had to be relevant to a contemporary audience.

Canada is fortunate in having many prolific and consistently excellent writers. In the interest of creating the broadest possible collection of works, we decided that an author would be included only once in a particular subject or genre. For example, Margaret Atwood, who could have had many titles on our list, is included once for a novel and once for a collection of poetry. This, we recognize, is an imperfect, but practical, limitation.

Practicality also dictated a limit to the number of titles. Most lists of this sort have one hundred titles. We chose 133, to symbolize Canada's age as a nation from Confederation in 1867 to the year 2000.

In undertaking this project, Vancouver Public Library pays tribute both to great Canadian works and to what professional librarians do every day by sharing their knowledge and love of books.

We encourage you to read the books on our list and to form your own opinions. If you make some pleasurable discoveries about Canadian writing and writers, then our project will have truly succeeded.

CHERYL RYLL
DIRECTOR OF MARKETING,
DEVELOPMENT & COMMUNICATIONS,
VANCOUVER PUBLIC LIBRARY

Acknowledgments

The Vancouver Public Library Board and staff wish to thank the following staff members who contributed to the creation and writing of this book:

Selection and Annotations Committee

Mary Ann Cantillon	Daniela Esparo	Anne Stockdale
John Cull	Yelena Kanevsky	Jane White
Corinne Durston	Diane Lorenzetti	Patti Wotherspoon
Ron Dutton	Donna Meadwell	
Mary Eaglesham	Cheryl Ryll	

Contributors

Helen Alexander	Anne Diano	Christina Gerber
Anne Bechard	Brooke Douglas	Natalie Gick
Stephanie Bohlin	Claudia Douglas	Peter Gourlay
Lin Brander	Janice Douglas	Glenda Guttman
Judith Brandon	Corinne Durston	Angela Haaf
Susan Buss	Ron Dutton	Holly Hendrigan
Karen Cannon	Mary Eaglesham	Jessica Higgs
Mary Ann Cantillon	Kirsty Elmslie	Patrick Hill
Janan Carr	Daniela Esparo	Deirdre Houghting
Terry Carr	Fred Faulkes	Sophia Karasouli-
Terry Clark	Lou Favelle	Milobar
Nancy Clegg	Tim Firth	Donna Kennerley
Olivia Craster	Shelagh Flaherty	Kristina Kumpf
Guy Cribdon	Lysanne Fox	Catherine Leach
John Cull	Anita Galanopoulos	Diane Lorenzetti

Lynne Macdonald
Bernadette McGrath
Janis McKenzie
Jeannie Ma
Donna Meadwell
Susan Meln
Jean Morris
Bill Nadiger
Amber Norcott
Lis Nygaard

Lindsey Pagnucco
Pauline Preston
Thomas Quigley
Maryte Racys
Surinder Reehal
Kate Russell
Nina Saklikar
Nicola Scudder
Nancy Singbeil
D'Arcy Stainton

Janet Tomkins
Musa Tryon
Richard Turner
Barbara Walker
Cathy Wang
Jane White
Patti Wotherspoon
Janet Wynne-
Edwards

We also extend a special thank you to staff members Ron Dutton and Fred Faulkes for their tireless dedication and commitment in preparing the final draft. Their effort and insight into the spirit of this project is a large part of its success. A heartfelt thank you also goes to Anne Stockdale, who initially brought *The New York Public Library's Books of the Century* and the idea for this book to our attention and who spent an epic amount of time preparing the final manuscript.

The Vancouver Public Library extends its sincerest thanks to Westcoast Energy for its financial support of this project and to *The Vancouver Sun* for assisting us with promotional support. We also sincerely thank CBC Radio and Television for their enthusiastic support of this project: "What a great way to celebrate Canadian culture! The Canadian Broadcasting Corporation of British Columbia, as part of our commitment to supporting Canadian arts and culture, is proud to promote this creative initiative of the Vancouver Public Library."

Last and certainly not least, we are most grateful to our publisher, Douglas & McIntyre, in particular Scott McIntyre and Saeko Usukawa, for their shared vision and enthusiasm.

THE

LAND

"Canada consists of 3,500,523 square miles of mostly landscape. It is apparently intended for the home of a broad-minded people."

members of the Group of Seven painters in an interview with

the *Belleville Daily Intelligencer*, 27 September 1919

The Journals of Susanna Moodie: Poems (1970)

Margaret Atwood

Susanna Moodie was an Englishwoman who, with her husband, emigrated to Canada in 1832 and homesteaded in the bush north of Toronto. The seven years they endured this hard frontier life were recorded by Moodie in her private journals. Later published as *Roughing It in the Bush: Or, Forest Life in Canada* (1852) and *Life in the Clearings Versus the Bush* (1853), Moodie's journals are now considered remarkable social and historical documents, as well as works of literature.

Poet Margaret Atwood is intrigued by the reluctant pioneer's feelings: Moodie alternately praised the Canadian landscape and bitterly complained about the bleak realities of bush life. Atwood sees parallels with contemporary views of the land: it is both wilderness and civilization, and we are often caught between resistance and acceptance, alienation and belonging.

This brilliant set of poems, inspired by Moodie's journals, uses precise language and tough, startling images to animate Atwood's vision of the Canadian psyche.

Mary of Mile 18 (1971)

Ann Blades

With the creation of *Mary of Mile 18*, Ann Blades became one of the first writers for children to portray a multicultural experience in a recognizable Canadian landscape. Little Mary Fehr thrills at the sight and sound of the wondrous Northern Lights. To her, they are a sign that something special will happen, and her discovery of a lost wolf-pup proves it. But Mary's joy is short lived. Reality for homesteaders like the Fehrs is that everyone must work to help the family survive, even a wolf-pup. The story of how Mary's little wolf earns its place within the family has made this book a favourite of Canadian children for over twenty-five years.

While children and adults respond to the timeless theme of a lonely child yearning for a pet, Blades also offers an engaging and authentic depiction of a close-knit Mennonite family struggling for survival in the harsh, frozen landscape of northern British Columbia. The unique beauty of Canada's bleak frontier and the relationships among the people who live there are successfully captured by Blades's naive and gentle watercolours.

The award-winning *Mary of Mile 18* is a true Canadian classic. It has also been translated into Swedish, Danish and German.

Return to the River:
A Story of the Chinook Run (1941)

Roderick L. Haig-Brown

R *eturn to the River* follows the life journey of a Pacific salmon named Spring. After her beginnings as a tiny egg securely hidden in the clean gravel of a Columbia River tributary, Spring swims down three rivers and through six hundred miles of Pacific Ocean north of the Queen Charlotte Islands (or Haida Gwaii), then retraces her route to return to that same gravel bed.

Along the way, Roderick Haig-Brown describes, in fascinating detail, each phase of Spring's life. Although the hazards that Spring faces, many of them caused by humans, foreshadow the disastrous collapse of the fisheries today, the tone is not discouraging, and the anglers and the fisheries biologists are treated with respect. Still, the reader cannot help but feel that the author would have been utterly surprised, and deeply saddened, by the fate of this great fish. In Haig-Brown's eyes, the salmon is the river itself, departing and returning in a cycle that no mere fish farm can duplicate.

Return to the River is a classic Canadian work of natural history. Haig-Brown was a well-known author, naturalist and conservationist. As a writer, he was posthumously honoured with the creation of the Roderick Haig-Brown Regional Prize for books, and as a naturalist and conservationist, with the establishment of a conservation area bearing his name, near the Adams River in British Columbia, where salmon come to spawn.

Historical Atlas of Canada

Volume I, From the Beginning to 1800 (1987)
R. COLE HARRIS, EDITOR; GEOFFREY J. MATTHEWS,
CARTOGRAPHER/DESIGNER

Volume II, The Land Transformed, 1800–1891 (1993)
R. LOUIS GENTILCORE, EDITOR; GEOFFREY J. MATTHEWS,
CARTOGRAPHER/DESIGNER

Volume III, Addressing the Twentieth Century, 1891–1961 (1990)
DONALD KERR AND DERYCK W. HOLDSWORTH, EDITORS;
GEOFFREY J. MATTHEWS, CARTOGRAPHER/DESIGNER

The physical characteristics of a land are inevitably linked to the accomplishments of the people who make their mark upon that land. In a country as vast as Canada, a historical atlas is essential to understand the relationship between human events and the geographical environment. As Cole Harris states, the atlas is a "report to the Canadian people about the nature of Canada."

In its three volumes, the *Historical Atlas of Canada* takes the reader from "The Last Ice Sheets, 18,000–10,000 B.C." up to "Canada in 1961." The double-page spreads, each devoted to a general topic or region of Canada, emphasize social, economic and cultural developments rather than the more traditional themes of political history, wars and boundary changes. The maps, graphs, diagrams, tables and illustrations are a joy to look at in their own right. These, combined with essays that range from archaeology and anthropology to sociology and women's studies, make the atlas an essential reference work that adds to the understanding of how and why Canada came to be what it is today.

The Group of Seven (1970)

PETER MELLEN

Peter Mellen's inspired study of the Group of Seven is clearly written, well researched and full of interesting diversions. The lives, works and ideas of the seven original artists and their associates are vividly woven together. The Toronto-based group's various intellectual concerns embraced theosophy, a vision for universal art education, and a collective search for a distinctly Canadian mystical identification with nature. Their self-congratulatory view of themselves as revolutionaries struggling against an indifferent establishment comes in for a gentle debunking at Mellen's hands. His research shows that despite one or two negative reviews of early shows, critical acceptance was quickly forthcoming.

The book itself is a well-crafted and innovative vehicle for art study. Elegant design by Frank Newfeld creates an almost seamless blend of text, art reproductions and photographs.

Jack Miner and the Birds, and
Some Things I Know About Nature (1923)

JACK MINER

A passionate naturalist and conservationist, Jack Miner devoted his life to studying the habits, life cycles and migratory patterns of birds. His early attempts to attract geese to his property in Kingsville, Ontario, led to the establishment in 1908 of one of the first bird sanctuaries in North America. He pioneered the banding of waterfowl to track their movements, and his research helped to establish the first restrictions on hunting waterfowl in the Migratory Bird Treaty (1917) between the United States and Canada.

In this, his first book, Miner writes with ease, humour and respect about woodpeckers, robins, bobwhite quail, ducks and geese, introducing readers to their habits, language and natural enemies—both animal and human. Describing the Canada Goose as one of the "most intelligent, self-sacrificing creatures on earth," Miner offers the story of a father goose mending a broken leg over the period of a month while tending to his family of eight.

Through his writings and lecture tours, Miner became internationally recognized as one of the fathers of wildlife conservation. In 1947, in its first unanimous vote since Confederation, the House of Commons established the National Wildlife Week Act in honour of Canada's famous "bird man."

Who Has Seen the Wind (1947)

W. O. MITCHELL

W. O. Mitchell's first and best novel is the sweet story of a
sensitive child's gradual awakening to the spiritual nature
of the world. The tale is set in the small Saskatchewan village
of Crocus, where every street-end disappears into the immense
solitude of sky and prairie. Four-year-old Brian O'Connal is
enchanted by the songs of larks and grasshoppers, the droplets
of water on the veins of a leaf. In this state of wonder, he yearns
to understand the thrilling shiver of the prairie wind on the
back of his neck.

At age twelve, the ever-curious Brian encounters both the
good and bad in life: the deaths of his father and grandmother,
the hypocrisy of religious zealots, the cruelty of children torturing
animals, conversations about the larger world with the school
principal and the local shoemaker. These vividly developed
characters and seemingly small, homely incidents change Brian
from an innocent child to one who learns that the wind can be
both the benign and menacing touch of God.

Mitchell's story is a perceptive dissection of small-town prairie
life, and very funny. This poetic book deserves its place on the
list of Canadian classics.

Owls in the Family (1961)

FARLEY MOWAT

The love of animals and nature is a hallmark of Canadian literature that features prominently in the works of conservationist Farley Mowat, who here writes as marvellously for children as he does for adults.

In this playful and at times poignant story, Mowat introduces young readers to the wonders of the Saskatchewan prairie and to the animals with whom we share the land. Set in Saskatoon, this is the story of two boys and their pet owls, Wol and Weeps. Wol is rescued from a storm-damaged tree, Weeps from an oil barrel. The narrative follows the boys and their owls on a variety of amusing escapades. Both birds have very definite personalities and soon gain complete control of their adopted human family.

Childlike and honest in style, *Owls in the Family* has delighted generations of Canadian children.

Canada: A Year of the Land (1967)

NATIONAL FILM BOARD OF CANADA

This attractive and large book—it weighs 4 kg (10 pounds)—
of beautiful photographs was the Canadian centennial
project of the National Film Board of Canada. An extravagant
publication, it was critically acclaimed and remains popular,
influencing and inspiring many other collections of photographs.

A *Year of the Land* features 260 plates, most of them in
colour, by seventy-seven photographers (Freeman Patterson and
John de Visser are well represented). The images are grouped
by season: Canada's many different springs, summers, autumns
and winters are recorded in their rich variety. The viewer is
whisked forward and back across the country, from "spluttering
little lobster boats tossing on Fundy's turbulent tide" to daffodils
"nodding prim and spinster-like in Vancouver's gardens."

Although the text is somewhat overwhelmed by the sheer
number of images, A *Year of the Land* stands as an evocative
contemplation of nature and the seasons, illustrating the
abundance and splendour, the familiarity and strangeness,
of the Canadian land.

As For Me and My House: A Novel (1941)

Sinclair Ross

Sinclair Ross's acclaimed first novel, a classic survival story, is set in one of Canada's harshest environments, the drought-stricken prairies. Events are related through the diary entries of Mrs. Bentley, the minister's wife in the small town of Horizon. An aspiring musician in her youth, she struggles to maintain her self-respect in spite of the daily hypocrisy forced upon her as the "minister's wife." She also struggles to break through her husband's coldness and indifference. An artist who turned to the church to make a living, he is barely able to cope with the repression that binds his life as a clergyman in a small town.

What enables the Bentleys to survive is their passionate belief in her music and his art. Their acts of creation allow them to transcend the literal reality of life and imbue it with meaning.

Ross's bleak prairie setting is both antagonistic towards his characters and symbolic of their inner struggles. The little town is nearly swallowed up by the immensity of its surroundings; only its false storefronts stand against the onslaught of the powerful winds. Dust and snow storms imprison the inhabitants in their houses, adding to the sense of entrapment.

This intense, complex work is one of Canada's most effective regional novels.

Where Nests the Water Hen: A Novel (1951)

La petite poule d'eau (French original, 1950)

Gabrielle Roy

translated by Harry L. Binsse

Franco-Manitoban author Gabrielle Roy won high praise for her first novel about life in a Montréal slum. But it is *Where Nests the Water Hen,* her lyrical second novel, that captivates hearts with its warmth of spirit, its beauty and its poignancy.

This novel is an intimate and graceful reflection of life in the northern Manitoba wilderness of the early 1930s. In the first part, a pioneer woman, Luzina, leaves her already large family to take what she considers to be her annual holiday, making the perilous yet exhilarating journey from Water Hen country to civilization to bear yet another child. The Water Hen region itself acquires the weight of a character with "its rustle of sedges, the beat of wings, the thousands of tiny, hidden, secret, timid sounds producing an effect in some way as restful as silence itself."

In the second part, Luzina, loyally supported by her husband, struggles with the backwardness of her surroundings and with the distance and anonymity of government bureaucracy, in order to bring education and opportunity to her family. The final part focusses on a character who complements and affirms Luzina's deep humanity, an amiable Capuchin missionary who travels the region encouraging justice, love, and a co-operative spirit among the ethnically and religiously diverse folk of these far-flung communities.

Gabrielle Roy's writing was deeply influenced by her life on the Canadian prairies and by the multicultural community that lived there. Deeper and more humane than her better-known *The Tin Flute*, this is an important Canadian novelist's best work.

Life-Histories of Northern Animals: An Account of the Mammals of Manitoba (1909)

Ernest Thompson Seton

Ernest Thompson Seton's early years were spent in Ontario and Manitoba, studying wild animals in their natural habitats. He believed that animals and humans were similar in many of their habits, behaviours and concerns, and throughout his life he tried to awaken others to a love of nature.

Seton pioneered a new genre of realistic nature stories written from the animals' points of view. Still enjoyed today, *Wild Animals I Have Known* (1898) illustrates the kinship of human and beast. Unlike the hunting stories popular in his day, these tales take readers into the minds and hearts of wild creatures.

Life-Histories of Northern Animals, Seton's first work of non-fiction, is based on over thirty years of observation. Filled with his own beautiful drawings and maps, it examines the habits, habitats and characters of sixty Canadian animals, from the red squirrel to the moose. Entertaining as it informs, the book interweaves the charming account of the beaver desperate for a mate, who wandered far and wide depositing mud-pies to advertise his availability, with facts on beaver populations and dam-building techniques. This is Canadian nature writing at its best.

Cedar: Tree of Life to the
Northwest Coast Indians (1984)

HILARY STEWART

Since the early 1970s, artist and writer Hilary Stewart has been exploring the material culture of the First Nations of the Pacific Northwest Coast. Cedar, the most important natural resource available to them, is examined here in all its detail. And such interesting and sometimes glorious detail it is.

There is a genuine enthusiasm animating the pages of this book. Stewart describes the geographical distribution of the species of cedar, red and yellow, with glances at the various legends associated with each. In drawings and in words, she explains various harvesting techniques, the tools required and the specific uses made of each part of the cedar. Every object traditionally made from cedar is included here: planks for huge houses, clothing and hats made from bark, massive dugout canoes, fish hooks, spirit whistles, ceremonial masks, monumental totem poles, large feast bowls and delicate spoons. The text is crisp and clear, but it is the hundreds of meticulously drawn illustrations that truly bring to life the book's subject matter.

Tom Thomson:
The Silence and the Storm (1977)

HAROLD TOWN AND DAVID SILCOX

There is perhaps no other painter who exerts the kind of romantic hold on the Canadian imagination as Tom Thomson. Dapper and good-looking, Thomson painted with intense feeling and died young under mysterious circumstances. His legacy was to demonstrate once and for all that a painter could take on the Canadian landscape and render it in a tone and style free of European and American trends. In 1917, such art was earth shaking.

This excellent book, marking the centenary of Thomson's birth, is an inspiring celebration of and a tribute to the artist's life and work. Some 177 high-quality reproductions of his paintings are presented, mostly true to their original size. The text by art historian David Silcox and artist Harold Town sketches in the known biographical facts, as well as the tales of legend. Silcox and Town also offer an acute critical commentary on how Thomson's rough gestural brushwork and exquisite use of colour influenced the aesthetics of painting in this country.

The Maestro: A Novel (1995)

TIM WYNNE-JONES

W hat could be more Canadian than Glenn Gould in a
northern setting? Here, Tim Wynne-Jones celebrates both
Canadian icons. The spirit and eccentricities of Gould the musical genius are embodied in the character of Nathaniel Orlando
Gow, a renowned composer working on a sweeping oratorio in his
remote cabin. Wynne-Jones draws on another of Gould's passions,
his love of the North, as he evokes the solitude and enigmatic
power of the landscape beyond Sudbury, Ontario.

When fourteen-year-old Burl Crow runs away from an abusive
father and a drug-benumbed mother, he stumbles upon Gow's
isolated cabin. Although he spends only a short time with the
composer, the boy is transformed by the experience. The
maestro, his music and the setting itself give the young Crow
the inner strength and insight to unlock his own tormented identity. The second half of the novel, with its urgent action and
suspense, brings an upbeat but far from sugar-coated resolution.

The Maestro, which earned the author his second Governor
General's Literary Award, represents Canadian storytelling for
children at its best.

A NATION IN

THE MAKING

"In older countries the future was inherited,

largely predetermined by the past.

Here, if we had the will, we could choose

what we would become."

journalist John Galt, in

Whistlestop: A Journey Across Canada, 1987

The Enemy That Never Was:
A History of the Japanese Canadians (1976)

KEN ADACHI

One of mainstream Canada's most cherished myths is that, except for the mistreatment of aboriginal people, our history has been relatively free from racial prejudice. This comforting notion is challenged by Ken Adachi's exposé, one of the first and best books to record injustices against Japanese Canadians, particularly during the era of World War II.

The book is a history of the struggles and achievements of the Japanese-Canadian community, from the end of the nineteenth century to the mid-1970s. Adachi's primary focus is the events provoked by public hysteria following Japan's bombing of Pearl Harbor on December 7, 1941. Between 1942 and 1949, almost 21,000 Canadians of Japanese descent were systematically dispossessed of their homes, property and livelihood. They were then relocated to internment camps in the interior of British Columbia and on the prairies. Adachi spent his teenage years in one such camp, and this first-hand experience gives his account a powerful immediacy.

Adachi lived to see the success of his work. In 1988, the federal government offered an apology and a compensation package to survivors of the internment camps, finally acknowledging one of Canada's more shameful historical episodes.

Confrontation at Winnipeg: Labour, Industrial Relations, and the General Strike (1974)

David Jay Bercuson

Turn-of-the-century Winnipeg was a terrible place for the working man or woman. The economy was based on the iron-working and metal trades—hard labour, often under deplorable conditions. Inflation, massive unemployment and the recent success of the 1917 Russian Revolution all added to the growing unrest. A wave of strikes rolled across Canada, nurturing the workers' dreams of One Big Union.

On May 15, 1919, labourers poured out of workplaces to gather on Winnipeg's main streets. Within twenty-four hours, they were joined by over 22,000 workers from the public utilities, post office and emergency services. For six tension-filled weeks, they held out for better wages, the right to collective bargaining and improved working conditions.

The General Strike was broken when Ottawa passed emergency legislation to deport "troublemakers" and to criminalize workers. The army was brought in, the mayor read the Riot Act, and the police fired into the crowd, killing one worker and wounding thirty others. Shockwaves from Canada's "Bloody Sunday" have reverberated through labour relations ever since, leaving a bitter legacy of mutual suspicion and class division.

David Jay Bercuson provides a skillful, if somewhat scholarly, narrative of this pivotal event in Canadian labour history.

The National Dream:
The Great Railway, 1871–1881 (1970)

The Last Spike:
The Great Railway, 1881–1885 (1971)

PIERRE BERTON

Canada's national identity is tied to the completion in 1885 of the Canadian Pacific Railway. The "ribbon of steel" crossed a 3200-km (2,000-mile) wilderness to connect isolated colonies. Stitching together diary entries, letters, newspaper accounts and government documents, Pierre Berton tells the exciting story in a sweeping, novelistic fashion.

The National Dream opens with the pledge by Prime Minister John A. Macdonald to build a railroad to the Pacific Ocean, an act labelled "insane recklessness" by his opponents. There follow ten years of political infighting, financial chicanery, and brilliance and bravery by the surveyors and engineers who map a railbed through the daunting landscape of muskeg and granite.

The Last Spike presents the dramatic five years during which the steel was laid. In addition to the rebellion in the Northwest and the terrible toll on Chinese workers, there was bribery, rapacious loan sharks, secret American bankers, land speculation and threats of imminent bankruptcy.

The books were instant best-sellers. Reviewers praised Berton's extensive research and captivating style, heralding him as the creator of a new Canadian mythology. Although academic critics dismissed Berton as a popular historian, these books changed the complexion of Canadian historical writing.

Northern Enterprise:
Five Centuries of Canadian Business (1987)

MICHAEL BLISS

Traditional accounts of Canadian economic history present grand visions of a country brimming with natural resources just waiting to be discovered by courageous explorers. Michael Bliss's monumental work distinguishes itself by disputing such conventional notions. His main premise is that Canadians and their governments have consistently overestimated the significance of the country's natural resources. He believes there has been no shortage of enterprise in Canada, but that it is "a harsh land, difficult to extract wealth from, and gravely handicapped by its small population and its peoples' and governments' great expectations."

Northern Enterprise covers the span of Canadian business from the first Atlantic fishermen in the 1490s to the Free Trade negotiations of the 1980s. The book has been widely praised for its panoramic scope, lively prose and controversial conclusions. Bliss merges anecdote and fact in a quick-paced survey. As the only one-volume complete history of Canadian business, it is an essential reference.

The Illustrated History of Canada
(1987, 2nd edition 1996)

CRAIG BROWN, EDITOR

This volume fills the long-standing need for a popular history of Canada that conveys just how big, how diverse and how rich our country's heritage really is. More than a traditional chronicle of parliaments and the powerful, the book presents a complex and modern sensibility. It incorporates the particular viewpoints of aboriginal peoples, ethnic minorities, women, tradespeople, farmers and fishers. Richly illustrated with maps, engravings, colour photographs and advertising posters, the book is lively, incisive and especially insightful about the harsh conditions under which we continue to build this nation.

The book begins with the meeting of alien cultures, First Nations and European, then traces the cross-fertilization and shifting balance of power as one group overwhelms the other. The story of New France describes how a separate and unique culture emerged in Québec, against a background of political conflict in Europe and at home. The section on the development of British North America details the colonization of regions outside central Canada and the building of national political, cultural and business institutions. The overarching theme here is the evolution of a nation from sea to sea, populated by distinct peoples who are still learning how to live with one another.

If you would like to know what the initials of the Hudson's Bay Company *really* stand for, or to read Jacques Cartier's first impressions of Canada, or to see what a World War II "Bren-Gun Girl" looked like, consult this readable and appealing volume.

The Canadian Encyclopedia
(1985, 2nd edition 1988)

JAMES H. MARSH, EDITOR-IN-CHIEF

In nearly every respect, this encyclopedia stands as a monumental achievement in Canadian publishing history. The three-
volume, 8,000-article, 3.2-million-word opus is the only Canadian
general encyclopedia produced since Grolier's *Encyclopedia
Canadiana* in 1957. Famous writers and experts such as Margaret
Atwood, Jack Granatstein, Farley Mowat, Margaret Ormsby
and David Suzuki are among the thousands of contributors. In
a country in which a book ranks as a best-seller if it sells 5,000
copies, Canadians snapped up more than 150,000 sets of the first
edition of *The Canadian Encyclopedia*.

The story of the book's creation is as epic as the work itself.
The brainchild of publisher, bookseller and unabashed patriot
Mel Hurtig, the encyclopedia owes its conception to his visit
to a school library in Swift Current in the early 1970s. Dismayed
by the lack of Canadian material on the shelves, he vowed to
create a reference source that would provide information on all
aspects of Canada. Funding proved a major challenge: Hurtig was
turned away by the Canada Council and all the major banks.
Finally, the Alberta government came through with a $4-million
grant, and the Canadian Commercial Bank offered a matching
loan. After more than a decade of planning, Hurtig published *The
Canadian Encyclopedia* in 1985 to glowing reviews and brisk sales.

The encyclopedia has since been revised, updated and
reissued in four volumes (1988). A French-language translation
was published in 1987 and a children's version, *The Junior
Encyclopedia of Canada*, in 1990.

The Unjust Society:
The Tragedy of Canada's Indians (1969)

Harold Cardinal

In 1969, the federal government unveiled its proposed new policy for the First Nations of Canada. In the name of Prime Minister Pierre Trudeau's "Just Society," Ottawa planned to repeal the Indian Act, dismantle the Department of Indian and Northern Affairs, and radically alter services to Native populations.

For twenty-four-year-old Harold Cardinal, the newly elected president of the Indian Association of Alberta, the time had come to speak out. An uncompromising Native voice was needed, someone who understood aboriginal peoples, the conditions under which they were forced to live, and the terrible impact these changes would have. More than a rebuttal to the government's proposals, Cardinal's book confronts Canadian society with its sorry historical record. Although aboriginal people were not massacred in Canada as they were in the United States, the appalling story of apathy and deliberate neglect does not make for comfortable reading. Cardinal describes the situation as bleak but not hopeless, and he presents a blueprint for change that offers First Nations people recognition and respect within a truly just society.

Cardinal's book had a tremendous impact on Parliament, on the press and on ordinary Canadians—it clearly touched an exposed nerve. Read it and decide just how far we have come in the past thirty years.

Folk Songs of Canada (1954)

More Folk Songs of Canada (1967)

EDITH FOWKE, LITERARY EDITOR

RICHARD JOHNSTON, MUSIC EDITOR

From "Alouette!" to "I'se the B'y that Builds the Boat," from "The Anti-Confederation Song" to "Red River Valley" and "The Maid of Newfoundland," we Canadians have always sung our lives, our geography and our history. Songs arrived on the lips of British, French, Scottish, Irish and American immigrants to harmonize with Indian, Inuit and Metis chants and tuneful narratives. Songs were sung on the land by farmers and cattle drivers; on the waterways by sailors, raftsmen, whalers and fishers; in the forests by lumberjacks and shantymen; in the mountains by miners and railway gandy dancers. We sang when we were sad ("White Man, Let Me Go"), in love ("Seventeen on Sunday"), dead drunk ("We'll Rant and We'll Roar"), or just feeling the need for a little gory humour:

> Oh, pity the cowboy
> All bloody and red,
> For his bronco fell on him
> And mashed in his head.

These two volumes offer the words and music for over 150 traditional Canadian songs, collected by esteemed folklorist Edith Fowke. Each song is arranged for voice, piano and guitar, and includes a short history with explanatory notes. Although the collections are works of serious scholarship, they are also handy sources for singing around the piano or the campfire.

Building Canada:
An Architectural History of Canadian Life
(1958, 2nd edition, 1966)

ALAN GOWANS

Have you ever wondered why Canada's cities have such a hodgepodge look to them? Alan Gowans's clearly written and well-illustrated history of Canadian architecture traces the complex interaction between cultures and architectural styles that has led to the appearance of our cities.

In a series of thoughtful essays, Gowans looks at the the shelters of stone-age times, the medieval building traditions brought from Europe to New France, the cabins and forts of pioneers, the eighteenth-century classical style, the American vernacular, the high Victorian, the neo-Gothic and, finally, the international styles of the modern era.

In addition to the importation of building styles, Gowans describes the peculiar psychology of Canadians, particularly a colonial mentality that saw greatness only overseas. He concludes that the result is not a great or even very original architecture. Instead, Canadians have freely adapted models from elsewhere to meet our needs at different times.

The book includes a lavish gallery of images, ranging from a Huron chapel made of saplings to a thatched Ukrainian-style farmhouse, as well as churches, water-mills, city halls, private homes and public markets. Together, text and illustrations present the fullest available chronicle of the development of Canadian architecture.

Lament for a Nation:
The Defeat of Canadian Nationalism (1965)

GEORGE GRANT

This book's influence has endured, even though it originated as a response to the defence crisis of 1963, when the government of John Diefenbaker refused to allow the United States to arm Canadian missiles with nuclear warheads. The Americans were openly hostile to Ottawa's decision, and soon the Liberal Opposition, the media and most of the Canadian establishment were calling for Diefenbaker's head. In their easy acquiescence, George Grant saw proof that Canada had become a mere branch plant of the American military-industrial machine. He lamented: "The society produced by such policies may reap enormous benefits, but it will not be a nation. Its culture will become the empire's to which it belongs. Branch-plant economies have branch-plant cultures."

With the book's publication, Grant became one of the first to raise the banner of Canadian nationalism, though it is not clear that such was his intent. In fact, he saw his book as documenting the *end* of Canadian nationalism. But in the rebellious milieu of the 1960s, the call to defend Canada's rights against American interference hit a nerve.

Today, the book's main themes still resonate with opponents of Free Trade and with people who feel alienated from the central Canadian establishment. This continuing relevance makes *Lament for a Nation* an important work thirty years after its first publication.

The Fur Trade in Canada:
An Introduction to Canadian Economic
History (1930)

HAROLD A. INNIS

This book has been described as the definitive study of the industry that played a crucial role in the growth of Canada. *The Fur Trade in Canada* was the first attempt to create a truly Canadian economic history. Harold Innis analyzed the distinctive character of our nation's development in terms of its geography and natural resources rather than relying on traditional British or American economic models (which he deemed inappropriate to the Canadian experience). His work came to be called "the staple theory of economic development": Canada's very existence was shaped by the staples (raw materials) that we produced for world markets, from fish, furs and timber to wheat, minerals and metals.

Although Innis was not the most elegant of writers—his prose is often swamped with unnecessary detail—his ideas were both groundbreaking and controversial. Contrary to other scholars of the day who asserted that Canada was a nation despite its geography, Innis insisted that Canada was a nation because of it. He believed this country exists naturally as a single, coherent entity, unified by a geographic structure that lies far deeper than mere political arrangements.

Innis was the first Canadian scholar to gain international academic status. His influence is still felt today, and his ideas continue to illuminate our understanding of the work-in-progress called Canada.

Economics (1966, 10th edition 1993)

RICHARD G. LIPSEY ET AL.

For beginners who are keen to learn the intricacies of economics, this college-level book is just the ticket. In straightforward language, Richard Lipsey introduces the workings of the marketplace, basic theories of supply and demand, price controls and monopolies. He explains the roles played by unions, governments, corporations, banks and international finance in the production and distribution of goods, as well as the great economic cycles and the theories that influence them.

The great strength of *Economics* is that, like its subject, it has evolved over time (thirty years of publication). Each edition has updated its examples to reflect changing conditions, world issues and new government policies. As an introductory textbook, it is unique because it does not skip over difficult issues and because it challenges readers to question theories where factual evidence is lacking or suspect. Well-organized and highly readable, this basic book on economics makes accessible an often arcane science that governs so much of our daily lives.

One of the most influential economists of the twentieth century, Richard Lipsey has produced a hugely successful work that has gone through many editions (with the help of other authors) and been widely translated. It remains the most comprehensive introductory survey of Canadian economic theory and practice.

The Trade Union Movement of Canada, 1827–1959 (1967, 4th edition 1978)

CHARLES LIPTON

The 130-year history of the trade union movement in Canada
is a complex saga of bitter strikes, hard-fought organizing
drives and legislative struggles. Charles Lipton's comprehensive
survey points out the milestones of the trade union movement
in a clear and forthright manner.

The story starts with the formation of local craft unions in
the 1820s and moves era by era into the age of the large industrial
unions. Lipton traces the influence of trade unionism and its leaders on the social, political and economic evolution of Canada.
Using both firsthand and secondary sources, he documents the
fight for better pay, shorter hours, safer working conditions, more
stringent child labour laws, political representation and the
creation of workers' compensation. References to developments
taking place at the same time in Great Britain and the United
States set the Canadian experience in an international context.

The book was first published in 1967, and the fourth edition
features an additional chapter on the long-standing tension
between the independence of Canadian unions and affiliation
with their counterparts in the United States.

The Story of Canada (1992)

JANET LUNN AND CHRISTOPHER MOORE
ILLUSTRATED BY ALAN DANIEL

P resenting history in a way that appeals to children without
distorting the facts is a challenge few authors have met.
In the case of Janet Lunn and Christopher Moore's *The Story
of Canada*, the achievement is monumental. Beautifully
designed and thoughtfully written, this history is stimulating in
its detail and appealing in its presentation.

Although the core of the book is the fluid chronological survey
of Canadian history, there are also dozens of intriguing sidebar
stories. As a taste, consider the fate of one eighteenth-century cow.
After the American Revolution had divided the continent into
two sides, Loyalists and Republicans, the cow was sold by a farmer
in Queenston, Ontario, to a farmer on the American side of
the Niagara River. Overwhelmed by homesickness, the animal
plunged into the river and swam home. In Queenston, they
called her the Loyalist cow.

The compelling narrative reflects both Lunn's talent as a
storyteller (she is also the author of two award-winning Canadian
historical novels for children) and Christopher Moore's background as an award-winning historian. The text is complemented
by the detailed illustrations of Alan Daniel, as well as by numerous photographs and reproductions.

Clearing in the West: My Own Story (1935)

Nellie L. McClung

Nellie McClung was, by the standards of any time, a remarkable woman. She was a mother of five, novelist, orator, suffragette, prohibitionist, reformer and one of the first female members of a provincial legislature in Canada. In addition, she was the first woman to serve on the CBC's Board of Governors and represented Canada at the League of Nations. After playing an energetic role in winning the vote for Canadian women, she toured the United States and Great Britain in support of suffrage. Her achievements are all the more remarkable since she had only six years of formal schooling.

In *Clearing in the West*, McClung tells the story of her homesteading journey from Ontario to Manitoba in the 1880s and ends with her marriage in 1896. Written in a charming and chatty manner, the book captures her memories picturesquely and with a flair for interesting detail. Young Nellie watches wagons disappear in the mud, notices uninscribed crosses marking graves along the trail, encounters howling prairie wolves, sadly observes the end of a massive buffalo slaughter.

McClung's sense of justice and the belief that women should have the right to vote are set against her mother's "old-world reverence for men." She reveals how her own independent spirit affected and shaped her as a teacher, and her attempts to get other women involved in politics.

Much more than a pioneer saga, this is the story of one of the leading figures in the worldwide movement for women's rights and perhaps Canada's most famous feminist. As such, it still deserves wide attention.

Two Solitudes (1945)

HUGH MACLENNAN

On the morning of January 17, 1945, *Two Solitudes* appeared in bookstores. By noon, the first print run of 4,500 copies had sold out, thanks to rapturous praise in the American and English-language Canadian press. The book remained on best-seller lists in both countries for the rest of the year, its success crowned by the Governor General's Literary Award for fiction.

Even though the book continues to sell well—worldwide sales are just reaching the million mark—the book is not an unqualified success as an example of the novelist's art. Its true merit is that it dared to set its drama in Canada and confront a genuine Canadian dilemma.

The story of Athanase Tallard and his half-English son, Paul, explores the uneasy relationship between Québec and the rest of Canada in the time between the two world wars. Although Paul's marriage to an anglophone symbolizes the mending of a nation divided, in retrospect the author's ethnocentrism looms large. The novel's message played well in the rest of Canada, but the Québec experience had already pegged intermarriage as the fast lane to cultural and linguistic assimilation.

Although its title has become a catchphrase for relations between Québec and the rest of Canada, *Two Solitudes* also pioneered a literature distinctly Canadian in subject, proving to other novelists that they could locate their stories here and still achieve artistic and commercial success.

Pélagie (1982)

Pélagie-la-Charrette: roman (French original, 1979)

Antonine Maillet

TRANSLATED BY Philip Stratford

Antonine Maillet is a multifaceted author who produces drama, novels, scripts, nonfiction and children's books. Born in New Brunswick and herself an Acadian, she has devoted her writing to Acadian life, culture, history and language; indeed, she is recognized as the first author to write in the distinctive Acadian dialect of French.

Using both fact and fiction, Maillet recounts the epic story of the widow Pélagie. In the decade after Acadians were forced to leave their Nova Scotia homes in 1755, she buys a rickety cart and leads a group of Acadians on a trek from the southern United States to return to their homeland. The novel is an affirmation of life, of the will to survive and of the spirit of Acadia. Pélagie has become a cultural heroine on a par with the Evangeline in Henry Wadsworth Longfellow's poem "Evangeline: A Tale of Acadie," which was also about the expulsion of the Acadians.

Pélagie-la-Charette won France's prestigious Prix Goncourt in 1979, the first time it was awarded to a non-European and only the sixth time that it was awarded to a woman. Unfortunately, no English translation could do justice to the lyricism and poetry of Maillet's original Acadian.

Canadian Establishment series

The Canadian Establishment, volume I (1975)
The Acquisitors, volume II (1981)
Titans: How the New Canadian Establishment Seized Power,
volume III (1998)

PETER C. NEWMAN

Peter Newman makes Canadian history and current events
not only interesting but exciting—and popular. *The
Canadian Establishment* (volume I of the series) sold three hundred thousand copies and staked a place on the best-seller lists
for fifty-four weeks. The book gave Canadians their first good
look at the one thousand men (there were very few women) who
controlled business in Canada, along with insights about their
great influence over the Canadian political scene.

The publication of violume II prompted lawsuits, and the
book was delivered to bookstores with one name blacked out,
making it all the more popular. *The Acquisitors* was about
new money and a fresh breed of entrepreneur, largely westerners,
who abhorred government intervention as much as they loved
big money and power.

Today, perhaps, we know too much about the rich and
famous, and *The Acquisitors*, especially, reeks of 1980s excess.
Nonetheless, these books provide a fascinating chronicle of
Canadian business personalities and history.

Newman is often faulted for being more of a storyteller than
a historian. However, great storytelling may be the reason over
a million copies of his books have sold in this country. His
dramatic style is backed up by extensive footnotes and bibliographies for readers who want more details.

The Vertical Mosaic:
An Analysis of Social Class and
Power in Canada (1965)

JOHN PORTER

John Porter's classic study of class and power ranks as the most influential and often quoted work of sociology ever published in this country. He spent eleven years researching how access to power within Canada is affected by social class, and his book contradicts the widely held belief that ours is a classless society. Although we live in a world different from that of Porter's time, the hierarchy he describes still excludes many from climbing "the vertical ladder" to power.

Born in Vancouver in 1921 to a single mother, Porter grew up knowing poverty first-hand. He left school in grade ten to support his family and only completed his education once he was demobilized after World War II. As he declared, "There is almost no one producing a view of the world which reflects the experiences of the poor and the underprivileged."

The Vertical Mosaic is essential reading for acquiring a historical perspective on the dynamics of class and power. It is a timeless work. As recently as 1998, some of Canada's top scholars reaffirmed Porter's findings in *The Vertical Mosaic Revisited*. There is much to gain from reading this original classic, which is still in print after thirty years.

Conspiracy of Silence (1989)

Lisa Priest

Late one November night in 1971, in the northern community of The Pas, Manitoba, a young Cree woman, living away from home while studying for her high-school diploma, was brutally murdered. Helen Betty Osborne was beaten, sexually assaulted, then stabbed fifty-six times with a screwdriver before being dumped in the bush outside town.

There was a carload of suspects, all white, their crime widely known within the town. Yet the case languished for thirteen years before the RCMP finally assigned a full-time investigator. Only two of the four perpetrators were ever charged. Their trial revealed a disgraceful succession of failings: slipshod crime-scene investigations, police intimidation of witnesses, backdoor immunity deals, community-wide racism and a conspiracy of silence.

News reporter Lisa Priest was just twenty-four years old when she wrote *Conspiracy of Silence*, in outrage at this case of blatant racism. The notorious case helped to trigger a public inquiry into discrimination against Native people in Manitoba. A meeting between Osborne's sister and one of the killers became Canada's first prison healing conference, in which the grieving family expressed loss and the murderer acknowledged his crime. But closure is not so easily had: this horrendous death and its reluctant resolution still cast a shadow over the Canadian justice system.

Rethinking Canada: The Promise of Women's History (1986, revised 1991, 1997)

Veronica Strong-Boag and
Anita Clair Fellman, editors

W omen's history is a relatively new area of study that focusses
on female perspectives that have been neglected in academic writing. *Rethinking Canada* redresses this omission with a
rich and varied selection of writings on Canadian women.
Twenty-seven essays from some of the best historians in the field
explore many subjects and periods from Canada's past: the lives of
women in New France and Loyalist eastern Ontario; the role
of Native women in the days of the fur trade; experiences in con-
vents and the Salvation Army; employment on dairy farms and
telephone exchanges; and accounts of immigrants, single mothers
and labour organizers. In all these selections, women play a
dynamic role, sharing the common bond of living and working
within a male-dominated society.

Rethinking Canada is an invigorating challenge to assump-
tions about race, sexuality, class, politics and social roles. This
book breaks new ground and is an excellent introduction to
a crucial aspect of our collective past.

Tales from Gold Mountain: Stories of the Chinese in the New World (1989)

Paul Yee

ILLUSTRATED BY Simon Ng

Graceful writing, beautiful design and stunning illustrations combine with memorable plots to make *Tales from Gold Mountain* an exceptional Canadian book for children. Paul Yee uses his knowledge as a historian and his personal experience as a boy growing up in Vancouver's Chinatown to breathe life into these eight stories.

Set on the West Coast, the tales reveal the hardships and triumphs that Chinese pioneers experienced during Canada's founding years. Whether encountering ghosts in a railway tunnel, cruelty in a salmon cannery or heartbreak on a farm, the characters prove resourceful and determined.

The stories read like folk tales. Some, like "The Friends of Kwan Ming" and "The Revenge of the Iron Chink," are about comic vengeance. Others tell of love and loyalty. All are memorable. The full-page paintings by award-winning illustrator Simon Ng are dramatic celebrations of these pioneers.

Tales from Gold Mountain was honoured with several prizes, and in 1996, another of Yee's books for children, *Ghost Train*, won the Governor General's Literary Award.

PORTRAITS

OF A PEOPLE

"Canada has never been a melting pot;

more like a tossed salad."

writer Arnold Edinborough in a speech at Chautauqua,

New York, August 3, 1973

I've Tasted My Blood:
Poems, 1956 to 1968 (1969)

MILTON ACORN
SELECTED BY AL PURDY

O n May 16, 1970, Irving Layton organized a gathering of some
of Canada's leading poets at Grossman's Tavern in Toronto.
There, they noisily proclaimed Milton Acorn "the People's Poet"
and presented him with an award of the same name, created to
honour *I've Tasted My Blood*. The book, they believed, had been
slighted by the Governor General's Literary Award committee.

Humankind, especially the common working person, is
Acorn's subject. He drew inspiration from the everyday world as
he found it: newspaper headlines, working-class friends, scientific
discoveries, armed revolutionary movements, Maritime history,
mythologies of the Great Goddess, even pop psychology. With
Dorothy Livesay, he was perhaps the most socially engaged
Canadian poet of his generation, believing passionately that
people are improvable and that injustices must be exposed. He
also held that social change is possible and necessary, and would
lead to a new and utopian world order. At the same time, Acorn
was a nationalist who wrote poetry to jar Canadians out of their
passive acceptance of the expanding American empire.

Al Purdy's superb selection of poems gathers much of Acorn's
best work, including "You Growing," which is regarded, like the
title poem, as a landmark of Canadian literature.

The Scalpel, the Sword:
The Story of Dr. Norman Bethune (1952)

TED ALLAN AND SYDNEY GORDON

A bon vivant and a brilliant surgeon, Norman Bethune joined the Spanish Republican freedom fighters in their heroic civil war against Francisco Franco's fascist army in 1936. In Spain, he pioneered the use of mobile blood transfusions on the battlefield. His last years were spent in China as a physician with the forces of Mao Zedong, opposing the Japanese invasion in World War II.

This biography focusses on the China period, promoting Bethune as a glorious internationalist hero: a romantic idealist dedicated to Communism and to science, a tireless worker who sacrificed himself to the cause of social justice. The book was not a popular success until the 1966 Cultural Revolution in China, when Chinese leader Mao Zedong's essay "In Memory of Dr. Norman Bethune" was one of three required readings for all Red Army cadre. Worldwide sales of the book soared to over two million copies in twenty languages.

Serious questions have been raised about the accuracy of the book's portrayal of Bethune. There is little documentary evidence to support much of the China material. Indeed, it was liberally cribbed from a 1948 Chinese novel, including a stirring—but fanciful—deathbed "last will and testament." Yet a wholly accurate account of this flamboyant, principled and often difficult man is probably beside the point. This impassioned biography does its duty as the foundation of a modern Canadian legend.

Breaking the Silence:
An Interpretive Study of Residential School Impact and Healing as Illustrated by the Stories of First Nations Individuals (1994)

Assembly of First Nations

From the mid-nineteenth century until 1975, Canadian aboriginal children were routinely removed from their homes to attend white-run residential schools. There, they were systematically deprived of their cultures, languages and family structures for assimilation into the alien Euro-Canadian society. Strict regimentation was frequently accompanied by emotional, physical, sexual and spiritual abuse. The result: generations of adults who are often filled with shame and who are culturally adrift and without hope, resulting in a continuing cycle of the breakdown of family and community.

Healing can begin only when these pain-filled facts are brought to light, and this book provides some essential exposure. *Breaking the Silence* is based on interviews with thirteen First Nations men and women, intercut with interpretive comments by psychologists Wilma Spearchief and Louise Million.

The book gives voice to the trauma and the loss suffered by these individuals. At the same time, it offers the wider aboriginal community strategies for survival, for healing and for reclaiming their heritage. For those who seek to understand one of the great tragedies in Canadian society, this book provides a crucial, first-hand perspective.

A Season in the Life of Emmanuel (1966)

Une saison dans la vie d'Emmanuel: roman (French original, 1965)

MARIE-CLAIRE BLAIS

By the mid-1960s, the young Marie-Claire Blais was firmly established as Québec's literary *enfant terrible*. Her stories and poems explored madness, murder, squalor, poverty and pain—especially children's pain—set within the tyranny of a repressive, insular society. Her characters were hate-filled, ignorant and often deliberately cruel. Blais was alternately praised as a brilliant but tormented literary genius, and damned as an amoral flash in the pan.

A Season in the Life of Emmanuel confirmed Blais's originality and importance to Québec literature. The story is observed through the innocent eyes of the newborn Emmanuel, sixteenth child of an impoverished, illiterate farmer and his beaten-down wife. The children dream of escape through religion, literature or work. In the course of a year, one by one they succumb to tuberculosis, alcohol, prostitution, thievery and fantasies of communion with the dead. Presiding over this spiritual destitution is the ferocious Grand-mère Antoinette, who survives by wielding her cane, her tongue and small bribes, avoiding victimization herself by mimicking the oppressive forces of nature, family and Church.

All this vile naturalist misery is redeemed from being grotesque—even ludicrous—by Blais's lyrical language, sustained use of fantasy and humour, and the tenderness with which she reveals her characters' toughness and suffering. Awarded the Prix Médicis, one of France's highest literary prizes, this remains one of her finest novels.

The Discovery of Insulin (1982)

Glory Enough for All: The Discovery of Insulin
(paperback edition, 1988)

Michael Bliss

Until the 1920s, diabetes was an incurable malfunction of the pancreas; its victims were debilitated by thirst, fatigue, skin boils and progressive weight loss. The preferred treatment of the time—a strict, almost starvation diet—helped few and killed many. The Canadian discovery of insulin saved millions of sufferers, including the inventor Thomas Edison, the writer H. G. Wells and King George V.

Michael Bliss meticulously documents the progress of discovery as it was stimulated by four highly charged, conflicting personalities. Frederick Banting, originator of the breakthrough idea for a cure, was a brilliant but insecure doctor with limited research skills. John Macleod, head of physiology at the University of Toronto, provided the extensive research facilities and experienced leadership needed to guide the project. A young assistant, Charles Best, was brought in to perform much of the complex testing. Ultimately, it was the skilled biochemist J. B. Collip who refined insulin to standards for human use.

The compelling tell-all story takes the reader through a maze of discovery and setback, ego and personality clashes, the jockeying for position on the team and credit for the discovery. In the end, the greatest public acknowledgement settled on Banting and Macleod, joint winners of the 1923 Nobel Prize for medicine.

This dramatic account makes a page-turning tale out of a great—perhaps the greatest—moment in Canadian medical history.

Ten Lost Years, 1929–1939: Memories of Canadians Who Survived the Depression (1973)

BARRY BROADFOOT

By the early 1970s, the Great Depression of the 1930s had been written off as an unhappy footnote in our nation's history: no one wrote or talked about it. Barry Broadfoot set out to rectify this situation, convinced that there were uniquely Canadian experiences to document.

Broadfoot's approach was simple. Criss-crossing the country with a tape recorder, he interviewed anyone with a story to tell about surviving the Dirty Thirties. Avoiding commentary, he lets people speak for themselves in thematic chapters that cover the barter economy, social unrest, hoboes, soup kitchens, home-made entertainments, offences against dignity and unexpected generosities. The stories are remarkable for their candour and their pain. There are tales of starving neighbours who simply disappear, of men working in backwoods relief camps for twenty cents a day, and of trains covered with men moving back and forth across the country—going nowhere. Taken together, the heart-break of the time is palpable.

Ten Lost Years reclaimed a painful but important chapter of Canada's past, and it struck a chord in Canadians of all ages. For those who had experienced the Depression, there was a kind of nostalgia for shared hard times. For baby boomers, there was a new understanding of their parents' view of the world. The best-selling book was eventually adapted as a highly successful stage play that toured the country and was broadcast on television.

The Hockey Sweater
(1979, illustrated 1984)

"Le chandail de hockey" in Les enfants du bonhomme dans la lune
(French original, 1979)

ROCH CARRIER
ILLUSTRATED BY SHELDON COHEN
TRANSLATED BY SHEILA FISCHMAN

It is the winter of 1946, and in the small Québec town of Ste-Justine, every boy's thoughts turn to pucks and skates. When Roch and his friends are not at church or at school, they play hockey, each wearing a replica of the Montréal Canadiens jersey of their hero, Maurice "the Rocket" Richard.

Life in Ste-Justine is circumscribed by religion. The village church stands guard beside the rink, and the children's beloved hockey games are refereed by the stern hand of God in the form of a black-robed curate. Young Roch and his friends are devout in their own way: they pray for God to endow them with the speed and skills of the Rocket.

When Roch's prized Canadiens jersey wears out, his mother orders him a new one from the English version of Eaton's catalogue. But what arrives in the mail is a Toronto Maple Leafs sweater, which he is forced to wear so as not to offend Monsieur Eaton. The persecution Roch suffers by donning Toronto blue instead of Montréal red is a poignant example of the regionalism that both defines and divides our country.

Sheldon Cohen's folksy illustrations complement the story perfectly. The book is a beautiful piece of Canadian heritage, and begs to be read aloud.

Conversations with Glenn Gould (1984)

Jonathan Cott

Universally acknowledged as one of the most brilliant pianists of the twentieth century, Glenn Gould was never less than provocative, even eccentric, in both his personal life and his music. After Gould's debut at age fourteen, his public career lasted a brief twenty years, during which he amazed, baffled and sometimes outraged audiences and professional colleagues. His startlingly unconventional interpretations of the classical repertoire revealed a witty musical explorer and a musician of "divine guidance."

By age thirty-two, Gould had retreated from the world stage to his solitary Toronto recording studio, believing that electronic media allowed for levels of clarity and immediacy seldom possible in live performance. A succession of superb recordings followed, while he continued to provoke the music world with lectures, magazine articles, self-interviews, radio and television narration, and compositions for film. His astonishing output is revealed and analyzed in this book of interviews.

Journalist and poet Jonathan Cott admits to being a star-struck fan of the pianist, as well as a friend and confidant. The book captures six hours of freewheeling telephone conversations between the two, ranging across Gould's musical habits, tastes and interpretations. We eavesdrop on his relationships with his pianos and audiences, listen to his delightfully lucid descriptions of musical passages, and watch him shed new light on his own legend.

Gould is compelling, passionate and sometimes loopy, but never dull. Perhaps the highest praise this book could receive is that Gould considered it to be the best interview he ever gave.

I Heard the Owl Call My Name (1967)

MARGARET CRAVEN

This evocative novel is both a lament for the slow ebbing of a traditional way of life and a parable of every human's quest for meaning.

Young Anglican priest Mark Brian is assigned to his first parish by a bishop who is privy to a secret the priest is not: Mark is terminally ill, with only two years to live. He is sent to an isolated, ancient Kwakiutl settlement known as Quee on the Pacific coast. Village life revolves around the cycle of seasons, patterns of animal behaviour, traditional ceremonies and the birth of children. This life is gradually collapsing, eroded by alcoholism, by traders and anthropologists who cheat the Kwakiutl of their remaining artifacts, and by children who have grown disenchanted with the old ways and are moving away.

As Mark slowly becomes part of village life, he comes to respect the dignity of a people watching the destruction of their world with sadness and resignation, and he learns to accept his own disintegrating health with courage. When, one winter evening, he hears the owl "call his name," Mark recognizes that he has reconciled his life and imminent death.

Avoiding sentimentality and simplistic blame, Margaret Craven shows Christian and Native worlds relating to one another where the issues are stark and suffering is real. Her thought-provoking, graceful writing draws strength from spare understatements, clear insights and deep-felt respect for all living beings. This first novel was an immediate best-seller in Canada, was widely translated, won literary awards and inspired a television movie.

Eagle Transforming:
The Art of Robert Davidson (1994)

Robert Davidson and Ulli Steltzer

Robert Davidson brings an impeccable family lineage to a Northwest Coast art tradition that values continuity and adherence to formal design rules. His great-grandfather Charles Edenshaw was a famous Haida carver, and his grandfather Robert was a noted canoe builder. By young Robert's day, this high art tradition had largely been abandoned, overwhelmed by European diseases, alcoholism and forced assimilation.

With encouragement from his father, at age thirteen Davidson was carving small figures from argillite, a glossy black slate unique to his home islands of Haida Gwaii (the Queen Charlotte Islands). Later, he studied with Bill Reid, an artist who played a large part in the revival of Haida traditions.

As documented here in Davidson's words and Ulli Steltzer's photographs, the Haida artist learned the rules of his art by first reinterpreting traditional images in flat designs for housefronts and storage boxes. Raven, Bear, Killer Whale, Wolf and Dogfish appear alongside his personal crest figures, Eagle, and his spirit helper, Frog. As his confidence grew, he increasingly incorporated his own artistic sensibility into prints, jewelry, totem poles, sculpture and ceremonial objects: masks, drums, rattles and bowls. Davidson's recent works address contemporary environmental and social issues such as the revival of the aboriginal fishery.

This twenty-five-year retrospective offers an intimate record of the life and work of a leading Canadian artist. It is a rare opportunity to observe the creative process and to learn the story of a personal journey that is part of the Haida people's cultural renaissance.

Jalna (1927)

MAZO DE LA ROCHE

Jalna is the first novel of the wildly successful Whiteoak Chronicles, a sixteen-volume saga that traces the fortunes and misfortunes of generations of a country family in Ontario. The novel opens in 1850, when a British soldier and his wife purchase a homestead in southern Ontario and begin building their estate, Jalna. The Whiteoaks are United Empire Loyalists, landed gentry whose elderly matriarch, the imperious Adeline, rules her family with an iron will. Her son Remy—sturdy, square-jawed, every bit the dashing romantic lead—oversees the estate under his mother's watchful eye. Adeline's many other children and grand-children are vivid personalities who lead lives of soap-operatic intensity as they weather star-crossed love triangles, financial troubles, love children, deaths and disasters.

Mazo de la Roche had been hailed as an important Canadian writer of serious realistic fiction for her earlier works. With the Jalna series, she moved on to unabashed romantic entertainment, well removed from reality and thin on social commentary. None-theless, her stories are strengthened by colourful rural settings and rich details of day-to-day Canadian farm life. Her creation is moving and memorable; as a whole, the Whiteoaks family is more fascinating than any of its individual members.

With phenomenal worldwide sales of over 12 million copies in 193 English and 92 foreign-language editions, the Jalna series remains among the most widely read of Canadian fictions. What accounts for this lasting public interest? Romance and family ties!

Up to Low (1982)

BRIAN DOYLE

Rarely is a story of healing and redemption found within the framework of a zany tall tale. This extraordinary novel for teenagers has a cast of unlikely, almost mythic characters: Crazy Mickey, Aunt Dottie, the Hummer, Mean Hughie and Baby Bridget. They are all part of a quirky odyssey that is equal parts slapstick comedy, Gothic horror, Ozark ballad and vision quest.

The adolescent narrator, Young Tommy, is on a family holiday with his father up to Low, a remote hill town in the Gatineau Hills near Ottawa. At each stop along the way, they hear that "Mean Hughie's got the cancer" and is dying. A violent, friendless man, renowned for slapping his child Baby Bridget in pure annoyance when a runaway binding machine cut off her arm, Hughie has disappeared into the bush to die. The novel follows Tommy and Bridget as they slowly fall in love and begin a search for Hughie that will end in confrontation, forgiveness, healing and death.

This seemingly grim story is enlivened by over-the-top characterizations and dialogue, its extravagant plot propelled by gags, scandal, sentimental ballads and the rambling anecdotes of adults overheard by Tommy. Ever threatening to veer out of control, the story is held firmly in place by Tommy's simple, almost naive narration and the author's skillful unfolding of the inner workings of his characters.

Considered one of Canada's most distinguished writers for young adults, Brian Doyle is here at his best, telling the tale of a remarkable summer in the 1950s when one Canadian youth learns that loving and healing are not always what they seem.

Leaving Home (1972)

David French

This drama takes place one tortuous evening in the late 1950s. The Mercers, a working-class family from Newfoundland living in Toronto, are getting ready for their youngest son's wedding. They soon discover that their other son is also leaving home in order to escape the constant tension with his oppressive father. Their fights are fuelled not only by a generation gap but by the clash between the regional and urban values represented by father and son. By the end of the evening, the father also leaves "home," surrendering his Newfoundland-based values together with his hope that they can be passed on to his sons.

David French drew from his own experience as a Newfoundland immigrant living in Toronto to write this, his first full-length play. A masterful portrayal of realistic characters in familiar predicaments, the work was produced in 1972 during a time of growing nationalism, when Canadian stories were in demand on the stage. An instant hit, *Leaving Home* helped to convince Canadian audiences that our own theatre was well worth seeing.

French has since written a number of popular and award-winning plays—including several in which he revisits Newfoundland and the Mercer family—that have been produced in Canada and abroad.

Paul-Émile Borduas (1988)

Paul-Émile Borduas, 1905–1960: biographie critique et analyse de l'oeuvre (French original, 1978)

François-Marc Gagnon

This is a major work about a major artist caught in the maelstrom of one of the truly revolutionary moments in Canada's history. Paul-Émile Borduas began his career in the 1920s, serving an apprenticeship to Québec's most famous church painter, Ozias Leduc. During the Depression, when such work dried up, Borduas resigned himself to teaching school. While he was observing how children create art spontaneously and imaginatively, Borduas experienced a moment of revelation that dramatically transformed his life. It propelled him to become one of the finest abstract and surrealistic painters of this century, exerting a profound influence on the development of painting in Québec. The experience also moved him to challenge the inwardly parochial views that had held Québec in cultural bondage for centuries. The *Refus global* manifesto (1948), a declaration of creative independence penned by Borduas and signed by fourteen other artists, was one of the opening shots in the province's Quiet Revolution. Borduas left Québec in 1953 and died in Paris seven years later.

François-Marc Gagnon, then professor of art at the University of Montreal, has written an exacting study of the artist's life and milieu. This hefty tome contains 147 full-colour plates, all beautifully reproduced, from the 1988 Borduas retrospective mounted by the Montreal Museum of Fine Arts. Gagnon provides major essays on each period of the artist's life as well as an insightful commentary on each painting.

Billy Bishop Goes to War: A Play (1981)

JOHN GRAY WITH ERIC PETERSON

Billy Bishop was a Canadian fighter pilot in World War I. He shot down seventy-two enemy aircraft and was awarded the Victoria Cross, our nation's highest recognition of military bravery. This play follows Bishop as he is transformed from a rural Ontario boy who joins the cavalry into a cool, ruthless killer in the air force. Along the way, he antagonizes his superior officers, tangles with the British upper class and has an audience with the king. At the end of the play, Bishop is a recruiter in World War II, still not understanding what World War I was all about, only knowing "it was a hell of a time."

The two-person musical was first performed in Vancouver in 1978, with playwright John Gray as the narrator and pianist. Eric Peterson played Billy Bishop and the sixteen other roles. The ambivalent desire for and fear of heroes that lies at the heart of Canada's quest for a unique national point of view made the play highly appealing.

Billy Bishop received the Governor General's Literary Award for drama in 1982. The play has been successfully produced over a hundred times across Canada.

Kamouraska: A Novel (1973)

Kamouraska: roman (French original, 1970)

Anne Hébert
TRANSLATED BY Norman Shapiro

Anne Hébert brings to her work a rich French-Canadian
tradition imbued with the influence and imagery of Emily
Brontë, Marcel Proust, Franz Kafka and James Joyce. Her literary
style was shaped by her village surroundings in rural Québec, by
her father, the noted poet and literary critic Maurice Lang-
Hébert, and by her poet-cousin, the still more famous Hector
de Saint-Denys Garneau.

Kamouraska, Hébert's second novel, with its universal theme
of tragic love, was immediately recognized as an evocative masterpiece of modern fiction.

The story is based on a true love-triangle murder that occurred
in 1840. As the tormented Elisabeth d'Aulières awaits the death
of her second husband of eighteen years, she ponders her life in
multiple flashbacks that have a dreamlike, at times hallucinatory,
quality. There is a disastrous first marriage, a passionate love affair,
a bloody murder, a trial—and a reprieve that gives Elisabeth a
superficial respectability. While watching her husband die, all of
her feelings of guilt build up. These mental horrors far outweigh
any real menace to Elisabeth's person and give the novel its
striking Gothic tone.

Winner of Le Prix des Librairies de France, *Kamouraska*
has been translated into German, Italian, Spanish and Finnish.
It was also made into a film by Claude Jutra.

Maria Chapdelaine:
A Tale of the Lake St. John Country (1921)

Maria Chapdelaine: récit du Canada français
(French original, 1916)

Louis Hémon
TRANSLATED BY W. H. Blake

Set in an isolated area of northern Québec at the turn of the century, this novel vividly depicts the traditional life of the French-Canadian habitant. Maria, the eldest daughter of the Chapdelaine family, attracts three suitors. The men are very different from one another—a dashing young *coureur de bois*, a wealthy American émigré and a neighbouring family friend—and Maria must choose the husband and the life that will best suit her. Maria's choices mirror those faced by Québec at a pivotal moment in its history. The process is entangled in a tragic series of events, but, in the end, the reader is left with the sense of a decision well made.

Maria Chapdelaine continues to generate lively critical interest both inside Québec and worldwide. The novel addresses the timely issues of urbanization and modernization versus the survival of traditional values and culture. Also, it is a very good read: a little romance, a few tears and a revealing picture of hardships endured by the farmers of the rocky Canadian Shield.

The novel has been in print continuously since it was first published, translated into some twenty languages, and been adapted for radio, stage, films—even comic strips and a popular song.

A Painter's Country:
The Autobiography of A.Y. Jackson (1958)

A.Y. JACKSON

A.Y. Jackson, one of Canada's more famous twentieth-century artists, was in his seventies when he wrote this anecdotal reminiscence of his life in art. All things considered, it was a momentous life. Jackson takes the reader from his early Montréal days to the art schools of turn-of-the-century Paris, through World War I, to his experiences as a member of the Group of Seven painters in Toronto. Although the Group of Seven was met by some initial scepticism—art of this sort will discourage immigration to Canada, one newspaper claimed!—the members persevered and gave the country its first original style of painting.

A *Painter's Country* is engaging and down-to-earth. The simple, fast-moving narrative is closer to oral history than formal autobiography. Humorous, honest and charming, the story is filled with many intimate sketch-portraits of the artists who dominated the Canadian scene during the first six decades of the twentieth century. The book also features twelve colour plates of Jackson's paintings.

Obasan (1981)

Joy Kogawa

*O**basan* is the first Canadian novel to document the treatment of Japanese Canadians after the bombing of Pearl Harbor in 1941. Naomi Nakane, a third-generation Canadian, is four years old and living in the relative security of a loving family. Events unfold through her eyes: she is an innocent who is trying to make sense of confusion and loss as anti-Japanese sentiment escalates around her. Naomi's aunt Emily, a second-generation Canadian, faces the situation head on, writing letters to Ottawa and speaking out for the community. Through Emily's letters and journals, the reader learns how the war has wounded the Japanese-Canadian community.

Obasan (the Japanese word for "aunt") is fifty when the story begins. She becomes the one constant for Naomi and her brother after their father is removed and they are relocated to to an internment camp in the remote Slocan Valley. When the war ends, they expect to return home, but instead are further displaced to the village of Granton, Alberta, where they labour on a beet farm. Throughout these hardships, Obasan bears her profound losses in silence. Not until Naomi returns to Granton as an adult can she begin to come to terms with their shared experience.

Joy Kogawa tells her story through flashbacks, with a lyrical style and acute observations that leave the reader with a deep sense of shame for the betrayal of a people. Remarkably, this was Kogawa's first novel. *Obasan* won the Canadian Authors Association 1982 Book of the Year Award, and the Books in Canada First Novel Award.

Baseball Bats for Christmas (1990)

MICHAEL AVAARLUK KUSUGAK
ILLUSTRATED BY VLADYANA KRYKORKA

Set in Michael Kusugak's childhood town of Repulse Bay, Northwest Territories, this gentle, poetic book relates the unusual fate of six Christmas trees that arrive by bush plane one December day in the 1950s. Having never seen trees before, the children ponder the purpose of the "standing-ups" and quickly realize, to their joy, that hidden under the pine needles and branches are new baseball bats. The whole of the following spring and summer, the community delights in playing baseball, hoping that Rocky Parsons, their bush pilot, will bring more bats the following Christmas.

Vladyana Krykorka, the Czech-born illustrator, has collaborated with Kusugak on many titles, all set in the North. Here, as always, she provides a series of lustrous drawings in a gorgeous palette of Arctic colours, enhancing the story and recreating on every page the sense of a happy, resourceful community. All six Kusugak-Krykorka collaborations are available in English, French, Inuktitut and Japanese. The exceptional quality of these books has done much to enhance the reputation of First Nations publishing.

Morrice: A Great Canadian Artist Rediscovered (1984)

G. Blair Laing

James Wilson Morrice, son of a well-to-do Montréal merchant family and a graduate in law, went to Paris in 1890. There, he was swept up by the great artistic innovators who were redefining the nature of painting: Degas, Cézanne, Toulouse-Lautrec, Monet, Renoir. It was an intoxicating milieu. Over the next six to seven years, he transformed himself into a master of the new forms and grew into a prominent and successful artist. Ever after, he called Paris home. He died in 1924.

Toronto art dealer Blair Laing began acquiring Morrice paintings in the 1940s and, over the course of his life, assembled a substantial collection. The desire to communicate his passion for the work of Morrice led him on an odyssey in search of the artist. This book is the result.

The ninety canvasses wonderfully reproduced here provide an immediate sense of what made Morrice so well regarded by the art critics of his day. With bold strokes that were the hallmark of the Post-Impressionist movement, a superb sense of combining colours and an ever-present sensitivity to the mood of the moment, Morrice was able to create an extraordinary body of work worthy of display in the great galleries of the world. Laing's tribute to Morrice is laudable, though it would be even better if his skill as a writer matched his heartfelt enthusiasm.

Sunshine Sketches of a Little Town (1912)

STEPHEN LEACOCK

These twelve short stories, created out of a series of newspaper columns in the *Montreal Star*, trace the follies and failings of the inhabitants of an imaginary Ontario town. In fact, Stephen Leacock drew much of his inspiration from the real-life folks in his hometown of Orillia. Although his readers chuckled at the comic realism of it all, the folks back home were a trifle miffed.

Leacock was keenly aware of the techniques that defined the British and American varieties of comedy. His exercises in gentle irony give his own style of humour a truly Canadian flavour. From his detached bird's-eye view, he softly sketches a town and its characters, inflating them with their own self-importance before deflating them with a wry but always affectionate bathos: "I can tell you the people of Mariposa are proud of the trains, even if they don't stop!" With Leacock, the punchline is never far behind.

These stories present a realistic though nostalgic portrait of a Canada caught between the pioneering past and the twentieth-century future. Although hugely successful at home, *Sunshine Sketches* never achieved the same level of popularity abroad as Leacock's other books, in which he employed foreign settings. *Sunshine Sketches*, then, is Leacock's great Canadian book.

Fall on Your Knees (1996)

ANN-MARIE MACDONALD

Not for the faint of heart, this richly textured saga of a Cape Breton Island family takes the reader on a breathtaking, epic ride from the coal-mining heart of the island to the European battlefields of World War I and into the burgeoning jazz scene of New York City.

After James Piper elopes with a young Lebanese girl, he spawns a family of four daughters, and what a cast of eccentric characters they are. James, giving in to his own darker impulses, sets in motion the events that will devastate the family. The eldest child, Kathleen, a gifted singer of great beauty, studies opera by day and Harlem jazz by night. Mercedes, the obsessively religious daughter, acts as a resentful mother to her two younger siblings. Frances, the wild and wayward rebel, selfishly panders to male weaknesses in a local speakeasy. Lily, the polio victim and adored angel, must in the end decipher all the terrible secrets that hide in the dark bosom of her family.

With great originality, Ann-Marie MacDonald proves herself singularly unafraid to tackle life's more unpalatable moments. She had already distinguished herself by winning the Governor General's Literary Award for her play *Goodnight Desdemona (Good Morning Juliet)*. For *Fall on Your Knees*, her debut novel, she won international praise and the 1997 Commonwealth Writer's Prize.

Hold Fast (1978)

KEVIN MAJOR

Kevin Major's debut novel concerns a young man who loses both parents in an auto accident and is sent from his village to the big city to live with an abusive uncle. The plot is fairly predictable young adult storytelling, but what makes Major's work stand apart is his insistence on writing in a strong, authentic Newfoundland voice. Descended from the Irish settlers, that spirit has clung to its inhospitable home for many centuries, learning to survive like the seaweed that holds fast to the pounded shore. This is the unique dialect of Newfoundland, fishers' profanity and all. Beyond the language itself is the novel's sharply drawn theme of day-to-day survival, which gives the story significance for many young people.

Among other honours, *Hold Fast* received the Canadian Library Association Book of the Year Award for Children in 1980. Major has since published six more titles for young adults.

Fugitive Pieces (1996)

<small>ANNE MICHAELS</small>

Poet Anne Michaels produced a literary *tour de force* with her first novel. The story concerns the young Jakob Beer, who escapes the Nazi slaughter of his family by burying himself in a Polish bog. Dug up and rescued by archaeologist Atmos Races, Jakob spends the war years in hiding on a secluded Greek island, haunted by memories of abandoning his beautiful sister Bella. Jakob's wounded spirit begins to heal under the spell of Races's tender care, in a precarious scholarly refuge of poetry, music, science and history.

The story then shifts to Ben, a young Canadian professor and himself the child of Holocaust survivors. Intrigued by the seemingly serene sixty-year-old Jakob, Ben travels to Greece to recover Jakob's notebooks and to learn how Jakob found resolution with his past.

Each man has a complex, many-layered history burdened with intolerable grief. Anne Michaels's strength is in revealing how lives interconnect in subterranean ways and how the human spirit can be consoled by time, trust and the power of language to witness and resolve.

This lyrical first novel became an immediate best-seller and garnered a number of international awards. Rich in poetry, memories, storytelling and brilliant imagery, the book confidently established Michaels's place in Canada's literary pantheon.

Lives of Girls and Women: A Novel (1971)

Alice Munro

Alice Munro's genius lies in her ability to portray the ordinariness of small-town Ontario life with a sharp, magical intensity. Winner of the 1972 Canadian Bookseller's Award, *Lives of Girls and Women* tells the story of Del Jordan, who is grappling with life's problems as she moves from the carelessness of childhood to the awakening sexuality of adolescence. Initially controversial because of its matter-of-fact treatment of female sexuality, the book has become one of the most highly regarded novels to appear in Canada.

Del's teen experiences are instantly recognizable: her dreams of becoming famous, embarrassment at her family's behaviour, humiliation over her body's development and subsequent delight in her experiments with love. Del is also a writer: her story is the portrait of an evolving artist as well as a delightful coming-of-age tale.

Munro, whose first book, *Dance of the Happy Shades*, won the Governor General's Literary Award for fiction in 1968, says that she is happiest when writing short stories. Indeed, *Lives of Girls and Women* is a hybrid: a novel that could also be described as a collection of linked stories. Munro has published several other works to general acclaim, winning the Governor General's Literary Award twice more. A sampling of her best short fiction from the past thirty years is available in *Selected Stories*, published in 1996.

The Guests of War Trilogy

The Sky Is Falling (1989)
Looking at the Moon (1991)
The Lights Go On Again (1993)

Kit Pearson

Meet Norah and Gavin, two characters so warmly and fully created that they readily became favourites with children and critics alike. In the award-winning *The Sky Is Falling*, Norah is ten and Gavin is five when they are shipped to Canada to escape the bombs falling on England in 1940. Placed with rich, strict Mrs. Ogilvie and her timid daughter, the young war guests find safety in Toronto, but not happiness. This is a perfect novel for nine to twelve year olds, with its sweeping emotional intensity and a plot enlivened with historical detail.

In *Looking at the Moon*, Kit Pearson captures the excitement and anxiety of Norah's thirteenth summer. She and Gavin are now comfortably part of the large Ogilvie clan and are spending a fun-filled month at the family's lakeside cottage. But heartache intervenes when Norah falls for sensitive older "cousin" Andrew and learns, through him, the moral dilemma facing pacifists in a world rocked by war and patriotism.

The Lights Go On Again describes the war's end and Gavin's reluctance to return home to England. After living in Canada for five years, he has formed strong attachments. It takes a visit from Grandad and a reunion with his ragged toy elephant to restore memories of his first home.

This fine trilogy was a success in the United States, Britain, Australia and New Zealand, and was also translated into French and German.

The Collected Poems of Al Purdy (1986)

AL PURDY

One of Canada's most popular and acclaimed poets, Al Purdy has dedicated his life to crafting poems in his singular style of colloquial erudition. Like Irving Layton and Milton Acorn, fellow modernists from Montréal in the mid-1950s, Purdy changed the way that Canadians write poetry. His earthy, anecdotal style and public persona as a self-taught, working-class "bad boy" contrast with the lyricism and spirituality of his work. Purdy's imagination and insight build a bridge between his regard for the past and his contemporary concerns. His influence on several generations of poets is considerable.

This collection spans four decades and thirty-two books, from Purdy's youthful attempts at traditional verse through years of apprenticeship to his emergence as a fully realized original artist. The book is not only an important milestone in Purdy's career but in Canadian letters.

The Collected Poems earned Purdy a second Governor General's Literary Award for poetry. The first was for *The Cariboo Horses* in 1965.

The Apprenticeship
of Duddy Kravitz (1959)

MORDECAI RICHLER

Many people will be more familiar with the movie version of *The Apprenticeship of Duddy Kravitz* than the original novel. In this coming-of-age story, young Duddy is an unscrupulous Jewish *pusherke* in Montréal, whose only aim in life is to be a somebody. His grandfather once told him that if you don't own land you're a nobody. Duddy takes this advice to heart and stops at nothing to achieve his goal. By the time he is finally able to purchase a piece of land, he has callously exploited his Québécoise girlfriend, betrayed his epileptic friend, and successfully eliminated all rivals with no apparent conscience. In the end, only Duddy's cab-driver father applauds him; his grandfather condemns his conduct.

There is very little to like about Duddy, yet there is something extremely captivating about his raw drive, vitality and shrewdness. This is tough and unrelenting social satire at its best.

The novel, when first published, was a critical success but a financial failure; it has since come to be regarded as a Canadian classic. Richler was named a Literary Lion by the New York Public Library in 1989, the same year he was awarded the Commonwealth Writer's Prize for *Solomon Gursky Was Here*, another fine example of his iconoclastic humour.

The Ecstasy of Rita Joe (1970)

George Ryga

This drama was a watershed in Canadian theatre, so thoroughly shocking and shaming its premiere audience in 1967 that they sat in stunned silence long after the cast had left the stage. It went on to win national and international accolades and remains a modern Canadian masterpiece.

The Ecstasy of Rita Joe traces the sad life of a young Native woman who leaves her reserve for the city and promptly finds herself on skid row. Poverty-stricken and despondent, she turns to alcohol and is soon arrested for a list of petty crimes: vagrancy, shoplifting, assault and prostitution. While sitting in court, Rita Joe recalls her bucolic childhood on the reserve with her family. She is unwilling to embrace either the passive traditional values of her father or the angry (yet equally powerless) radicalism of her boyfriend. Some time after they are betrayed and disappointed by unhelpful white "liberals" such as the Priest, the Teacher, the Indian Centre and the Judge, Rita Joe and her partner are brutally murdered.

George Ryga wrote many other plays and two novels, all similarly committed to voicing hard truths about the poor and downtrodden members of society.

Les Belles Soeurs
(The Sisters-in-Law) (1974)

Les belles-soeurs (French original, 1968)

MICHEL TREMBLAY

TRANSLATED BY JOHN VAN BUREK AND BILL GLASSCO

Fifteen women who live in Montréal's East End spend an evening together, pasting a million trading stamps, won by one of them in a contest, into booklets. By the end of the night, what began as a gathering of friends has degenerated into an all-out battle for possession of the stamps.

This black comedy was considered radical (and controversial) when it was first produced on stage. Written entirely in *joual*, the slang dialect of Québec, the play presents a naturalistic view of French-Canadian life, a view not entirely appreciated in all corners of Québec society. Tremblay and his characters pull no punches in this challenge to Québec social myths and conventions. Unlike the stereotypical ideal of the cheerful Québécoise wife and mother, these women are neither joyous nor contented: feelings of helplessness have made them intolerant of everything and everyone. Trapped in lives they despise, they lack even the ability to recognize, let alone express, their discontent.

Internationally acclaimed, *Les Belles Soeurs* has been translated into many languages and been performed around the world. Although Tremblay wrote the play with a Québécois audience in mind, its themes of alienation and entrapment are universal.

The Double Hook (1959)

SHEILA WATSON

In this intense story set in the Cariboo region of British Columbia, Sheila Watson uses short, spare sentences, down-to-earth vocabulary and abrupt cadences to create a distinctive Canadian sound. The large questions facing the remote community at the heart of this story, however, are on a mythological level. Eddying around the novel's central event—the mysterious death of a family's matriarch—are primal themes: the search for hope amid despair, sacrifice as a prelude to redemption, rebirth as a conclusion to death. This interplay of dark and light at the heart of human existence is represented by the "double hook"; as Watson writes, "When you fish for glory you catch the darkness too."

The Double Hook holds a special place of honour in the development of Canadian fiction. Many critics consider it essential reading, although some readers will find the heavy symbolism a bit daunting. It is important for being the first truly modern novel written in Canada.

Swamp Angel (1954)

ETHEL WILSON

Ethel Wilson was born in the confines of the Victorian age, and the twentieth century was already half over before she published her first novel. She flourished then for some fifteen years, publishing seven books. *Swamp Angel* is her best known and certainly most impressive novel.

The book's central character is Maggie Lloyd, a woman who abandons a distasteful second marriage for a new life as a cook at an isolated fishing lodge in the interior of British Columbia. Three Loon Lake, superficially beautiful yet treacherous below the surface, symbolizes all of life's ambiguities. Maggie discovers strength in the compassion she finds herself showing to those around her. Her ability to rise above circumstances is sharply contrasted with her eccentric friend Nell's lifelong obsession with the "Swamp Angel"—the handgun that the older woman used in a circus juggling act.

Although Wilson's literary output was both modest and out of step with other writers of the time, her distinctive, regional voice and sense of place have earned her a place in the literary canon of British Columbia and Canada.

NEW

PERSPECTIVES

"I don't explain—

I explore."

media theorist Marshall McLuhan, in

McLuhan: Hot and Cold

The Edible Woman (1969)

Margaret Atwood

With this first novel, Margaret Atwood, who was already a noted poet, established herself as a significant Canadian prose writer. It is the deliciously funny story of Marian McAlpine, a young woman on the verge of marriage, whose sane and structured life is gradually crumbling. She is horrified to find herself progressively less able to eat: first meat, then eggs and even vegetables nauseate her as she comes to identify with each food. The condition worsens as, relinquishing control of her life to her conservative fiancé, she fears that she herself is being consumed. Marian's struggle to become herself again is played out in humorous subplots with a casual lover and a partying roommate.

Critics have variously described *The Edible Woman* as a classic comedy, a witty and brilliant satire on the politics of male-female relations, and a feminist tract. Atwood's language is vivid, her sharp comic sense shines throughout, and her characters are colourful, well rounded and true to life. The book has retained its relevance to women's lives and their changing role in society, remaining a valuable contribution to women's fiction.

The Griffin & Sabine Trilogy

Griffin & Sabine: An Extraordinary Correspondence (1991);

Sabine's Notebook: In Which the Extraordinary Correspondence of Griffin & Sabine Continues (1992);

The Golden Mean: In Which the Extraordinary Correspondence of Griffin & Sabine Concludes (1993)

NICK BANTOCK

No one could have predicted that this quirky adventure in publishing would top the best-seller lists for years. Although the story is at heart an old-fashioned romance through letters, Nick Bantock presents it in an interactive and highly sensual form. Real postcards and real letters in envelopes are glued into the book, giving the reader the pleasurable shiver of opening someone else's mail. The beautiful and highly imaginative images range from surreal collages to Leonardo da Vinci–style notebook jottings to exquisite postage stamps.

The text relates in words what the art reveals in images. Griffin Moss, a lonely London postcard artist, and Sabine Strohem, a mysterious postage stamp artist in the South Pacific, gradually fall in love through their correspondence. Throughout, Griffin is haunted by the suspicion that this woman may be just a figment of his psyche. Enigmatic to the end, the story concludes with a sharp shock.

Bantock draws upon the best of children's literary traditions to create this series of adult picture books, in which story and image entwine as closely as lyric and melody.

The Comfortable Pew:
A Critical Look at Christianity
and the Religious Establishment
in the New Age (1965)

Pierre Berton

In 1963, the Anglican Church of Canada asked Pierre Berton to write a book to serve as Lenten readings. The Church had entered a period of self-examination and felt that the views of an outsider would stimulate discussion. Berton had free rein to write what he pleased and to expand the scope of the project to include other established Protestant churches.

He did just that. Berton ranges widely across social issues, dispensing scathing judgements on the churches' self-satisfaction and smug indifference to injustices. He queries their complicit silence during the massive peacetime buildup of lethal nuclear arms. He examines clerical passivity in the face of widespread racial bigotry and corporate misconduct. And he judges the churches to be politically conservative, theologically ignorant and increasingly irrelevant in a world that learns its ethics from television.

A torrent of news articles, editorials and rebuttals followed the book's publication. Church reactions ranged from stung outrage to agreement that the problems were of long standing and worthy of thoughtful address. The public was intrigued: unprecedented sales made *The Comfortable Pew* the best-selling book on religion ever published in Canada.

David and Other Poems (1942)

EARLE BIRNEY

After six months of receiving enough rejection slips to paper a wall, Earle Birney finally succeeded in having *Canadian Forum* magazine publish his debut poem, "David," in 1940.

The narrator and his friend, David, go mountain climbing in the Canadian Rockies. All is well until an accidental fall leaves David paralyzed from the neck down. Acquiescing to his friend's plea, the narrator throws David to his death from the mountain ledge.

Two years later, some of Birney's poems were published in book form, and they were immediately hailed for their originality and intensity. The book went on to win the Governor General's Literary Award for poetry in 1942. Some unwary readers, convinced that the title poem, "David," had a real-life basis, urged that Birney be arraigned for murder. In the contrasting descriptions of the topography—*inspiring* before David's fall, *sinister* afterwards—Birney encapsulates the strangely contradictory attitude Canadians often hold towards our majestic landscape.

At once a dedicated, professional writer and a restless experimentalist, Birney tried his hand at most literary forms— novels, short stories, verse and radio plays, and literary criticism. He is widely acknowledged as English Canada's finest poet.

The Wealthy Barber:
The Common Sense Guide to Successful
Financial Planning (1989)

DAVID BARR CHILTON

Financial planning is not everyone's favourite bedtime reading, so Chilton makes it appealing with a basic, folksy plot. Every month, a fictional barber meets in his shop with four young customers who want to increase their wealth. Instead of intimidating charts and graphs, the barber gives financial advice in the form of anedcotes, comments on his students' efforts over the past month and assigns new tasks. Covering such topics as insurance, RRSPs, taxes and estate planning, investment in homes and real estate, savings, budgets and mutual funds, the barber promotes a "pay yourself first" strategy to set aside 10 per cent of net income.

The book caught the imagination of Canadians, many of them baby boomers who wanted a short and understandable guide to navigate the turbulent waters of personal financial management. It quickly became a publishing sensation, with over a million copies in print—not bad for a self-published book whose first seven thousand copies were sold out of the author's garage.

Stranger Music:
Selected Poems and Songs (1993)

LEONARD COHEN

For every romantic who has ever longed to spend the night with Leonard Cohen, this collection of almost three hundred poems, song lyrics and short prose pieces should make compelling reading.

Hailed somewhat disparagingly by the popular media as "the grocer of despair," Cohen has paraded a consistent and, dare we say, narcissistic eroticism throughout his forty-year career as poet, singer and novelist. Although his work reveals scattered traces of political, religious and philosophic awareness, it is anguish that supplies the unifying poetic ingredient. The need for love is constant, but here, love is rather impersonal, possession by the beloved is strongly resisted, and the predictable outcome is the solitude from which anguish is reborn. And so, round and round it goes: longing, resistance, solitude, longing...

Although Cohen's writing is animated by some expert poetic control and a wry charm, much of his poetry is single-minded in its pursuit of sensuality. North American critics, with their somewhat heightened feminist sensitivities, have been less kind to Cohen-the-poet than those in Europe, where his popularity as a balladeer has been very high for thirty years.

In the Sleep Room:
The Story of the CIA Brainwashing
Experiments in Canada (1988)

ANNE COLLINS

Beginning in the mid-1950s, psychiatrist Dr. Ewen Cameron performed brainwashing experiments on patients at Allan Memorial Institute in Montréal. He was convinced that he could develop reprogramming techniques to cleanse troubled minds of disturbing thoughts and behaviours. His method, called "psychic driving," included massive amounts of electro-shock, coma-inducing drugs such as LSD coupled with endless repetitive messages, sleep deprivation—even surgery—in an effort to break down his patient's psyches.

Anne Collins's exposé has two parts. The first, an account of twenty years of brutal human experimentation, makes wrenching reading. The disastrous effects on patients—nightmares, depression, suicide, brain damage and emotional death—are gruesome and heartbreaking.

The second part details the frustrating attempts by 9 of his estimated 332 victims to obtain accountability and justice. For many years, Cameron's work was secretly funded by the United States Central Intelligence Agency, which was pioneering mind control as a Cold War weapon. When the CIA lost interest, the Canadian government took over sponsorship of Cameron's work. This tale of government complicity and evasion is well documented and shameful. Only after the book's publication did Ottawa and Washington provide victims with compensation.

In the Sleep Room won the 1988 Governor General's Literary Award for non-fiction and was adapted as a television miniseries.

The Baby Project (1986)

SARAH ELLIS

Sarah Ellis's award-winning debut novel is a realistic and compassionate portrayal of a family's struggle to cope with the tragic death of a new baby. The narrator, eleven-year-old Jessica, is the youngest member of the Robertson family. After learning that her mother is expecting, Jessica and her best friend embrace the idea by turning a school science project on the life cycle of the duck-billed platypus into a study of babies: "the baby project."

The first half of the novel is a witty, episodic look at the Robertsons. Ellis paints a picture of a modern family juggling the challenges of working parents, teenagers and an approaching birth. But when baby Lucie succumbs to sudden infant death syndrome, the novel becomes a thoughtful exploration of grief and the family's gradual recovery.

Reviewers and readers have praised Ellis for her sensitive treatment of serious themes and for her skill in creating well-rounded, believable characters. In *The Baby Project*, Ellis achieves a fine balance between humour and tragedy that makes this an important contribution to contemporary Canadian children's literature.

In 1991, another book by Sarah Ellis, *Pick-Up Sticks*, received the Governor General's Literary Award for children's literature in English.

The Wars (1977)

Timothy Findley

This novel is the mature work of Timothy Findley, a leading Canadian author. The story, set during World War I, is a variation on a time-honoured theme: the journey of an innocent through suffering to heroism.

The story is told in documentary realism, through tape-recorded interviews, press clippings, old photographs, diaries and letters gathered by a historian and archivist. Robert Ross, the son of a wealthy Toronto family, goes to war gladly—it is at once a glamorous adventure and a release from oppressive memories of a family tragedy. At the battle of Ypres, he is initiated into the terrible reality: this is a war bogged down in stinking grey mud and rain, run by the incompetent and the corrupt. A second war rages within him, one that both forges his personality and destroys it through a sense of futility and too much experience of death.

The Wars is a daring blend of fact and fiction, poetry and prose. A literary achievement as well as a powerful statement about war, the novel received both the Governor General's Literary Award for fiction and the City of Toronto Book Award.

Unidentified Human Remains and the True Nature of Love (1990)

Brad Fraser

P laywright Brad Fraser first came to critical attention in 1986 with this bleak, edgy drama about the complexities of contemporary love. David and Candy are roommates, ex-lovers and best friends. David avoids genuine emotional attachment by choosing a rootless life of waiting on tables and risky, anonymous gay sex. Candy believes in love but never quite gets it right, and inevitably ends up hurt by both her male and female partners.

The play is a comedy, a horror story, a romance and a farce. After opening lightly with a cascade of smart, funny dialogue, the atmosphere quickly darkens. Somewhere in the city, a serial killer is murdering and mutilating women. One of David's buddies regularly turns up at his apartment, bloodied from some backstreet fight. The clairvoyant prostitute next door specializes in sex with violence and recites monstrous urban legends about stalking and terror. Yearning for genuine connection and community, these tentative, damaged characters offer one another confused emotional support in an increasingly sinister setting.

With this extraordinary play and its successors, Fraser re-creates the voice and viewpoint of Generation X. At once cynical and romantic, fearful yet in-your-face, cocky but incomplete, the play embodies the attitudes that we are carrying into the new century.

Fraser scripted an excellent film adaptation of his play, under the title *Love and Human Remains*, in 1995.

The Affluent Society (1958)

John Kenneth Galbraith

In this book, John Kenneth Galbraith set out proposals that he gleefully predicted would irritate just about everybody. They did: both the left and right wing were outraged. Conventional economic wisdom assumes that a healthy economy calls for continued growth through ever-increasing production of goods. Galbraith contends that this idea leads to the manufacture of unnecessary and unwanted products, which the public is then persuaded to buy through advertising. This frantic spiral of rising production, wages and prices causes abrupt swings between boom and bust, as well as degrading the quality of life and the environment.

Galbraith proposes redirecting all this energy to increased public services and government control of key industries. He advises slowing down economic growth, lowering personal consumption and taking time off work to smell the roses.

One of the great economists of the twentieth century, Galbraith has influenced government policy for four decades. His witty, persuasive, down-to-earth and often biting style has captivated readers. Economics, often called "the dismal science," has rarely been so provocative and entertaining. Of the thirty-odd books he has penned over the years, several were best-sellers, including *The Affluent Society*, which remains in print and continues to excite debate.

Reflections of Eden:
My Years with the Orangutans
of Borneo (1995)

Biruté M. F. Galdikas

With gentle humour and sharp wit, Biruté Galdikas, the world expert on orangutans, has written an engaging book about her life and her study of the "red apes." In fact, her life and her work prove to be one and the same.

The narrative begins with a description of her family's Lithuanian roots, and she skips over most of her Canadian childhood. The real story begins in Los Angeles, where she meets the famous scientist Louis Leakey, who helps her to realize her dream of studying orangutans. The reader then journeys with the young Galdikas to the steamy rain forests of Borneo and is introduced to her adopted family, the great apes.

Galdikas's passion for her subject is infectious. Her captivating accounts of these gentle giants are a riveting mix of scientific facts and vivid profiles of individual orangutans. As she grows older, the changes in her life are reflected in the changes that affect the lives of the orangutans to whom she is so dedicated.

For over twenty years, Galdikas has been an observer of, and an advocate for, the orangutans of Borneo. Her fascination with these animals persists, and she continues to perform groundbreaking research. Sometimes seen as a thorn in the side of the Indonesian government, she is a leader in the fight to protect the now endangered orangutan and the rapidly disappearing rain forest that is its home.

Neuromancer (1984)

William Gibson

American-born William Gibson, who has lived in Canada since 1968, took the science-fiction world by storm with the publication of this first novel. The first volume of a trilogy, it was followed by *Count Zero* in 1986 and *Mona Lisa Overdrive* in 1988.

The central character in *Neuromancer* is Case, a cowboy of the future, a computer hacker hired to plug a digital version of his mind into cyberspace and, once there, to steal data. The novel describes a dark, dystopian world dominated by global capitalism, in which outlaw hackers like Case hide out in industrial ruins, trying to outwit Japanese corporations. Combining the raw energy and cynicism of hard-edged rock music with the powerful influence of high technology, *Neuromancer* was hailed as the harbinger of a new type of writing dubbed "cyberpunk," after the term "cyberspace" that Gibson himself coined to describe the vast reaches of digitized information.

Neuromancer was the first book to sweep all three of the major science-fiction awards—the Hugo, the Nebula and the Philip K. Dick.

Fortune and Men's Eyes (1967)

JOHN HERBERT

> When in disgrace with fortune and men's eyes,
> I all alone beweep my outcast state,
> And trouble deaf Heaven with my bootless cries,
> And look upon myself, and curse my fate
>
> WILLIAM SHAKESPEARE, SONNET 29

In the late 1940s, John Herbert was convicted on a morals charge and was sentenced to six months in Guelph Reformatory. What he learned there is captured in the Shakespearean title of this gritty play. The prison is a mirror of the larger, equally corrupt society that degrades and brutalizes its members until they lose contact with their humanity.

The naive Smitty enters a prison world whose distorted values accommodate racism, blackmail, assault and homosexual rape. His moral choices quickly narrow to survival strategies, represented by the violent and manipulative Rocky, the gently disassociated Mona and the hardened comic, Queenie. Cunning and cold-blooded aggression are necessary to ensure self-preservation. Love—even compassion—can seem an unacceptable risk.

Fortune and Men's Eyes is the most popular of Herbert's fourteen plays, some of which remain unpublished or unproduced. It has won most of Canada's major theatre awards and was adapted to film in 1971. The drama has been produced in at least forty languages in well over a hundred countries. One of its lasting legacies has been to inspire Fortune Societies for prison reform in several countries.

The Keeper of the Isis Light (1980)

MONICA HUGHES

Considered one of Monica Hughes's best books, *The Keeper of the Isis Light* is the first volume of a science-fiction trilogy for teens. On the beautiful, distant planet of Isis, the only inhabitants are the robot lighthouse keeper, Guardian, and the orphaned sixteen-year-old Olwen, who has been genetically altered to adapt to the planet's harsh, hot climate. Olwen is in harmony with her environment and is unaware of her isolation. Her beauty mirrors the planet's, but settlers who arrive from Earth are horrified and awed when they see her without a mask. In the end, they all reject Olwen, including seventeen-year-old Mark, who had initially befriended her. Wounded but proud, Olwen withdraws, now aware of her solitary state but still at one with Isis.

Hughes, a newcomer herself, reflects upon the Canadian immigrant experience when she describes the seclusion of Isis, the struggles of settlers on an unfamiliar planet and their clash with its inhabitants. Her strong, compassionate and very human character of Olwen has a universal appeal.

Guardian of Isis (1981) and *The Isis Pedlar* (1982) complete the trilogy. Hughes's numerous literary awards include the Canada Council Children's Literature Prize in 1981 and 1982.

The Bias of Communication (1951)

Harold A. Innis

"The conditions of freedom of thought are in danger of being destroyed by science, technology, and the mechanization of knowledge, and with them, Western Civilization." Harsh criticism of the Bill Gates empire? Could be, but in fact the words were penned almost half a century ago by a political economist born in Otterville, Ontario.

Applying his complex "time-space" concept of how media affects the ability of civilizations to solve problems, Harold Innis argued that the then new electric media of telegraphy and radio were so powerful (maximum space) but so preoccupied with immediacy (minimum time) that they totally undermined our ability to create long-term solutions to our problems. All this, before faxes, e-mail and the Internet.

Media theorist Marshall McLuhan said that Innis studied his sources with the sensitivity of a Geiger counter. Innis's deep reading led to impressively deep thinking. Unfortunately, he rendered his deep thoughts in a highly compressed writing style that does not permit ready understanding. As a result, he inspired almost no following in his own time. His genius may be to inspire new schools of thought in centuries to come.

The Death and Life
of Great American Cities (1961)

JANE JACOBS

In this critical challenge to post-war urban renewal practices, Jane Jacobs proposes that the social and economic diversity found in the older neighbourhoods of large North American cities are the lifeblood of these communities. Then the editor of *Architectural Forum* magazine, she was appalled at the social damage done by wrecking balls, which ushered in the dreadfully uniform housing blocks that were intended to remove the blight of poverty from the urban landscape. As experience has shown, this simplistic and monotonous approach only multiplied the social problems of older neighbourhoods.

Jacobs's passionate insights presented real alternatives to the prevailing thought of the time. The book received a mixed welcome in its day. Academic critics, keen to protect their turf, were unsparing; British critics found the study, with its east coast American slant, too limited. However, others appreciated her engaging prose and recognized the much-needed corrective to the disastrous shortcomings of contemporary city planning. Jacobs is credited with revolutionizing the way many North Americans view their cities.

Portraits of Greatness (1959)

YOUSUF KARSH

The brooding photographs in this book form a highly inter-
pretative visual archive of the great faces of two decades,
1940 to 1960. Yousuf Karsh, the Armenian-Canadian photog-
rapher, set up shop in Ottawa in the '30s and went on to create
some of the most compelling portraiture of his day. The ninety-
six photographs in this collection clearly demonstrate his unique
style: an almost crushing darkness, set off only by the sharply
defined light on the faces of his subjects.

Karsh had a little boy's idolizing fascination with those who
had truly excelled in some field of endeavour, especially when
the endeavour conformed with European notions of high culture
in the arts, academia or politics. More importantly, he had a
rather shrewd sensitivity to a subject's guardedness, and he worked
out subtle strategies to bring down that guard. It was often when
his sitters ever-so-briefly exposed their more fragile inner selves
that Karsh clicked the shutter.

Special paper and soft inks were used to reproduce the
photographs in the book. Many of Karsh's portraits have come
to represent the way these hero-figures are viewed in the popular
imagination. Brief biographical captions on his subjects plus
longer reminiscences about the day of the shoot by Karsh
himself accompany each photograph.

Shoeless Joe (1982)

W. P. KINSELLA

W. P. Kinsella came to professional writing late in life—he was in his early forties when his work was first published. An editor at Houghton Mifflin saw a story that Kinsella had contributed to an anthology and was so impressed with "Shoeless Joe Jackson comes to Iowa" that he suggested Kinsella turn it into a full-length novel. Shoeless Joe was a real baseball player who, along with his teammates from the Chicago White Sox, was banned from the game after throwing the 1919 World Series. The novel *Shoeless Joe* appeared in 1982 to generally rave reviews.

In this idiosyncratic story, dreams, the will to believe, love, wonder—and the power of the imagination to transcend reason and time—all act together to raise baseball from the mundane to a timeless reality. A voice tells Ray, a young Iowa farmer, to destroy a large portion of his corn crop in order to build a baseball diamond: "If you build it, they will come." And they do. The early legends of baseball return from the dead, yet the effect of these events is far from Gothic and much more akin to inspirational. This Canadian-born author captures the American spirit of baseball in a way that no American fiction writer has yet matched.

Shoeless Joe attracted a readership well beyond hard-core baseball fans and was successfully adapted for a popular movie titled *Field of Dreams*.

The Diviners (1974)

MARGARET LAURENCE

The last of Margaret Laurence's Manawaka cycle of novels, *The Diviners* won the Governor General's Literary Award for fiction in 1974, despite an initially lukewarm reception. The book has also faced tough challenges in some school jurisdictions on the grounds of obscenity.

The Diviners does make an odd first impression, being superficially awash with characters and situations animated by far too many narrative devices.

In the critical rereading of the novel, its true worth comes to light. Morag Gunn, the central character, is a writer and mother struggling with the conflict between her own needs and the demands of others. In the complex weave of stories, the reader sees that Morag is not alone. As much as Morag may articulate her life from the inside out, those things outside her—family, townspeople, photographs, newspaper articles, songs and letters— articulate her from the outside in. The narrative's constantly shifting point of view, which initially discomfits the reader, is now considered to be the source for much of the novel's strength and originality.

Like the river that opens and closes the story, life, as Laurence portrays it, is a stormy, ever-changing backward and forward movement. Breaking free of convention to find her place in the rhythm and flow of life is Morag's ultimate salvation. In this way, too, *The Diviners* has found its own ongoing salvation.

A Wild Peculiar Joy:
Selected Poems, 1945–82 (1982)

IRVING LAYTON

Irving Layton was born in Romania in 1912 and emigrated with his family to Montréal one year later. In the early 1940s, he fell in with the city's literary crowd and began seriously writing poetry.

Layton gained popularity (and notoriety) in the 1950s by shattering the conventions that constrained Canadian poetic practice. Until then, no one had published such personal, fervent and exuberant poems. He was a lusty, brawling socialist from the Jewish ghetto, shaking his fist at puritanism and timidity. Wrenching Canadian poetry from the genteel preserve of academics, he turned it into a more streetwise form that broke taboos regarding language, subject and style.

A Wild Peculiar Joy includes many of Layton's greatest poems. "Bull Calf" (1956) describes, with pity, the slaughtering of a newborn calf. "Keine Lazarovitch: 1870–1959" (1961) is a moving elegy to his mother, a fierce and stubborn woman. "Grand Finale" (1978) is Layton's version of Dylan Thomas's "Do Not Go Gentle into that Good Night," as well as a self-mocking rebuttal to his critics.

Layton's champions claim he has written some of the most powerful poems in the English language, while his critics focus on his egomaniacal personality. The following generation of poets, including Margaret Atwood, Al Purdy, Gwendolyn MacEwen and Leonard Cohen, owe much to him. Layton won the Governor General's Literary Award for poetry in 1960 and was nominated for the Nobel Prize in Literature in 1982.

From Anna (1972)

JEAN LITTLE

Jean Little delivers an emotion-packed story that explores Anna's childhood in an immigrant family. After witnessing the Nazi treatment of his Jewish friends in pre-war Germany, Anna's father fears for his family's future and decides to move to a new life in Toronto.

The story is told through Anna, a sensitive child who is trying to find her own place within her family and in her new world. The uprooting is the most painful for Anna, and her difficulty in learning to read makes her feel especially isolated, awkward and vulnerable. The discovery of Anna's visual impairment, her new glasses, and her placement into a special class mark the start of her touching journey toward self-discovery and confidence.

From Anna is based on the author's own childhood struggle with visual impairment and vibrantly displays her ability to bring to life children with different abilities and immigrant backgrounds. Anna's story has moved the hearts of generations of Canadian children and helped them to identify with children who are different from themselves.

Jean Little is one of Canada's most well-known and best-loved children's authors, and her books have been widely translated. She has received many honours, including the Canada Council Children's Literature Prize, the Canadian Library Association Book of the Year Award, the Ruth Schwartz Children's Book Award and the Order of Canada for her outstanding contribution to children's literature.

The Shadow-Maker (1969)

GWENDOLYN MACEWEN

A prolific writer of fiction, drama, travel and children's books, Gwendolyn MacEwen is best remembered as one of our most gifted and popular poets. She dedicated her life to writing, publishing her first poem at the age of sixteen. Outwardly, MacEwen's work reflects her fascination with ancient civilizations, religion and myth; inwardly, she explores the source of the life force within the unconscious mind. This set her apart from other Canadian writers, misleading some critics into labelling her work as "exotic," yet MacEwen's spellbinding and riveting poetry defies such categorization.

The Shadow-Maker is representative of MacEwen's quest for a deeper understanding of life. Bouncing off Carl Jung's "It is 'a fearful thing to fall into the hands of the living God,'" she writes in the opening poem, titled "The Red Bird You Wait For":

> Its name is the name you have buried in your blood,
> Its shape is a gorgeous cast-off velvet cape,
> Its eyes are the eyes of your most forbidden lover
> And its claws, I tell you its claws are gloved in fire.

Her art lies in magically using simple language, strong rhythms and vivid imagery to express the shadow-mysteries of life and of dreams. MacEwen's work won two Governor General's Literary Awards for poetry, in 1970 and in 1987, the year of her untimely death at the age of forty-six.

The Medium Is the Massage (1967)

Marshall McLuhan and Quentin Fiore
Jerome Agel, co-ordinator

This is a short, witty and still timely book by Canada's most famous—some would say infamous—commentator on the effects of electronic media on our sense of self. Published over thirty years ago when Marshall McLuhan was at the height of his fame, the book is intentionally provocative.

The media guru's controversial words are set with typographical frenzy within a jungle of images. The book is fun, too, simulating the printed word's loss of status to the more engaging electronic media as the major force shaping our critical thinking. For the neo-tribal baby-boom generation of the 1960s, the book was a real happening. More sober minds saw *The Medium Is the Massage* for what it was: an entertaining romp through McLuhan's irrational visionary mind.

The Nature of Managerial Work (1973)

Henry Mintzberg

What does a manager actually do? In this pioneering study, one of the all-time great management gurus provides insights and answers to the question while offering his theories of managerial work.

Based on observations of five managers over one week, Mintzberg's study challenged the traditional scientific management theories of the 1950s and 1960s. He discovered that management decisions are grounded not in theories but in human communication in its many forms: the manager's many, often very brief, daily encounters and conversations with individuals.

The book is surprisingly readable. When first published, it was hailed as a welcome addition to a subject area better known for quantity than quality. Mintzberg himself has won national and international acclaim. He was the first Fellow of the Royal Society of Canada to be elected from a management faculty, and twice received the McKinsey Prize for the best article in the *Harvard Business Review*.

A Fine Balance (1995)

Rohinton Mistry

As an immigrant from India living in Canada since 1975, Rohinton Mistry tells a tale that has both an insider's intimacy and an outsider's objectivity. The four main characters are caught in a grinding moment of India's history. Dina Dalal is an impoverished young Parsi widow, struggling to maintain her independence by working out of her home as a dressmaker. Into her cramped quarters moves an indifferent student, just arrived from the countryside. Hoping to expand her business, Dina hires two tailors who are striving to break out of the straightjacket of their low caste. The stories of all four are told against the ominous backdrop of Indira Gandhi's 1975 declaration of a State of Emergency, a measure designed to divert public attention from the corruption of her government.

The four become a family of sorts, experiencing together the world's abundance of sorrows: venal landlords, crooked bureaucrats, lying politicians, brutal police and shrewd crime bosses. To capricious politicians, "urban renewal" means razing the hovels of the poor, and "population control" means forced sterilization. The only holdout against this misery, injustice and inhumanity is the human spirit and its ability to maintain a fine balance between hope and despair.

Despite its monumental 748 pages, the narrative rushes compellingly forward, a harrowing story constantly redeemed by moments of generosity, integrity and humour. The novel's scope and ambition have been compared with the work of Dickens, Narayan, Joyce, Rushdie and Balzac, and won for the author Canada's prestigious Giller Prize.

Sea of Slaughter (1984)

Farley Mowat

In a voice as bitter and relentless as the book's theme, Farley
Mowat recounts the long history of the exploration and
exploitation of the Atlantic coast of North America. For over five
hundred years, people have overfished, trapped, polluted and
encroached upon habitats; today, we are left with little more than
frail traces of ecosystems that once teemed with life. This horrify-
ing record of mindless, often deliberate destruction, leaves readers
overwhelmed by sadness, loss and anger. Like Rachel Carson's
Silent Spring, Mowat's book is an attempt to make us aware of
the precious, fragile world in which we live.

In the past, critics have accused Mowat of providing insuffi-
cient evidence to support some of his claims, yet he remains a
leader in the conservation movement, as well as an internationally known author whose books have sold millions of copies
worldwide. Written in his characteristic storytelling style, *Sea of
Slaughter* and other works such as *People of the Deer* (1952) and
Never Cry Wolf (1963) have helped to focus public attention
on environmental concerns.

The Paper Bag Princess (1980)

ROBERT MUNSCH

ILLUSTRATED BY MICHAEL MARTCHENKO

Once upon a time, there lived a beautiful princess. One day, a dragon blazes through her castle, leaving her with nothing but a paper bag and the memory of her beloved prince being carried off in its fiery clutches. Putting on the paper bag, the brave damsel sets off in pursuit. The princess outwits the dragon and rescues her not-so-charming prince—an undeserving prince, she decides, as she skips merrily into the sunset, alone.

This modern twist to the conventional fairy tale quickly became a Canadian best-seller. Robert Munsch's first collaboration with illustrator Michael Martchenko created a lasting image of the feisty Princess Elizabeth and launched a partnership that has spanned eighteen years and produced twenty-two titles. Many of Munsch's stories pass the "read it again" test before they are ever published. Oral versions of the stories are tested on preschool audiences; their enthusiastic responses to Munsch's spirited and resourceful child characters have no doubt contributed to his considerable success.

Today, Canada's best-selling author has 30 million copies of his books in print. His stories have been translated into eleven languages and are the basis for sound recordings, animated and live-action video recordings, television specials and CD-ROMs. *The Paper Bag Princess* remains a favourite, alongside the hugely successful *Love You Forever* (1986), which topped the *New York Times* list of all-time best-selling children's books in 1994.

The Canadian Inventions Book:
Innovations, Discoveries and Firsts (1976)

JANIS NOSTBAKKEN AND JACK HUMPHREY

So you know all about James Naismith and J. Armand Bombardier of basketball and snowmobile fame, but have you ever heard of Thomas Carroll or James Miller Williams or Gideon Sundback? Of these three, can you say which one invented the modern zipper? Which one invented the "Miracle of the Harvest"—the world-famous self-propelled combine that did the work of two or three hundred field labourers? Which one drilled the world's first oil well? Do you know who John Patch is, and what he sold for a bottle of rum and a keg of flour?

If you know the answers to these questions, you've probably already read *The Canadian Inventions Book*.

For the first book to popularize Canadian ingenuity, the authors unearthed an inspiring array of inventions and inventors. Instead of publishing a comprehensive list, Janis Nostbakken and Jack Humphrey chose people and creations they found appealing, then assembled fascinating anecdotes, asides and trivia, along with pages of cartoons, drawings and photographs. The result is a highly entertaining and enlightening book of Canadian firsts.

The Collected Works of Billy the Kid: Left Handed Poems (1970)

Michael Ondaatje

Best known for his extraordinary novel *The English Patient*, Michael Ondaatje's first foray into fiction is this unusual work. *The Collected Works of Billy the Kid* is historical fact rearranged to create a seemingly simple yet potent mix of monologue, verse, prose, captionless image and pictureless caption. Anecdotal and conversational in tone, the story is charged with a rhetoric that rips the reader out of the here and now. In language that cuts to the bone, Ondaatje shows us a desperado-killer who nevertheless communicates an existential kind of humanity. The book's spare hundred or so pages move Billy from the primitive, unforgiving Old West landscape to the moment of his death — a point where fear ends and the self becomes transcendent.

Winner of the Governor General's Literary Award for prose and poetry in 1970, *The Collected Works of Billy the Kid* went on to be published in the United States in 1974 and was later adapted as a play.

The English Patient: A Novel (1992)

MICHAEL ONDAATJE

Poet and novelist Michael Ondaatje roguishly blames the tropics (he was born in Sri Lanka) for shaping his shimmering literary style, where the real and the imaginary fuse. Memory stores badly, he claims, like everything else in the tropical heat: it blurs. Ondaatje experiments with overgrown images and blurred genres in his explorations of culture and race that underlie the very human stories in three novels, *Coming Through Slaughter* (1976), *In the Skin of a Lion* (1987) and *The English Patient*.

This last novel focusses on a quartet of soul-scarred characters who, as World War II draws to a close, find sanctuary and healing in a ruined villa in Tuscany. Hana is a Canadian nurse traumatized by war and the recent news of her father's death in battle. She remains behind the lines to nurse a severely burned soldier, known only as the English patient. The two are joined by a friend of Hana's father who was once a thief and spy but is now suffering from injuries inflicted by Nazi torture, and by Kirpal Singh, a Sikh British Army lieutenant who is an expert in defusing unexploded mines and bombs.

Within their wartorn world, the characters develop a fragile intimacy and friendship based on shared confessions, memories and experiences. Ondaatje's ability to convey the strength of the human spirit in finding love in the midst of adversity has won him recognition as a major international author.

The English Patient won the Governor General's Literary Award for fiction in 1992, and was co-winner of Britain's Booker Prize. The book was turned into a brilliant film.

Home: A Short History of an Idea (1986)

Witold Rybczynski

The nature of house and hearth has changed considerably over the centuries. Just how much is the subject of this thoroughly researched and highly readable study. Although Witold Rybczynski does an admirable job pointing out the social, economic and technological forces that have shaped those spaces we call home, the book's animating force is the search for what constitutes the comfort zone. "During the six years of my architectural education the subject of comfort was mentioned only once," Rybczynski begins. He claims that the matter of comfort is too important to be left to the self-proclaimed experts like architects and interior decorators, who have led us to the wide open spaces of the modern home where function and efficiency may reign but where coziness gets short shrift.

With its witty, conversational tone and exquisite style, *Home* is that rare find—a book that doesn't seek so much to instruct as to make the reader aware. There is information aplenty here, but it is the theme of comfort that gives the book its appeal. The answer to the question of what makes a comfortable home, Rybczynski wisely leaves up to the reader.

The Stress of Life (1956)

HANS SELYE

Stress is one of the curses of modern life. Hans Selye not only originated the concept of stress, he advocated a revolutionary idea that many consider to be among the most important medical discoveries of the early twentieth century: that stress plays a role in human illness. He found that stress plays a part in *every* disease. In addition to the obvious effects on people's emotions and mental health, Selye describes how stress can influence the development of high blood pressure, ulcers and other illnesses.

The Stress of Life places Selye's ideas before a mainstream audience in a charming anecdotal style that is free of the pomposity that marred most scientific writing at the time. Selye not only popularizes his research but outlines the intricate process that scientists go through to prove or disprove their theories.

Since the book was first published, theories of stress have changed slightly, but *The Stress of Life* remains an excellent explanation of the subject.

By Grand Central Station
I Sat Down and Wept (1945)

ELIZABETH SMART

When a maverick English publisher brought out this intense, painful autobiographical prose poem in 1945, the author's mother persuaded Prime Minister William Lyon Mackenzie King to confiscate and burn any copies that might stray into Canada. The fact that this was duly done to the six copies that made their way across the Atlantic speaks eloquently of the effectiveness of our Customs department.

To the chagrin of her family, Elizabeth Smart, an Ottawa debutante reared in the sensibilities of the *petite* aristocracy, had slipped into the full-fledged London bohemianism that she was to assiduously cultivate her whole life long. *By Grand Central Station I Sat Down and Wept* is a searing though metaphorically guarded exposé of a woman overcome by her own obsessive love for a man. In real life, that man was poet George Barker, who was married at the time, an inconvenience that did not dampen Smart's ardour. The relationship was to produce four children for Smart and gave her a rather battered sense of self. Her deep longing to reveal all, combined with an obvious need to shroud, resulted in an exquisitely crafted landscape full of muted metaphors and muffled allusions. For the reader, the story is a resonant testament to the ways of the unruly heart.

The Art of Mary Pratt:
Substance of Light (1995)

Tom Smart

If a painted image of a block of Emmenthal cheese in plastic wrap or eviscerated chickens in butcher paper or cod fillets in aluminum foil turns your art-appreciation crank, read on. Mary Pratt, the painter responsible for these and other domestic scenes, showed early talent. She attended Mount Allison University, studying under such luminaries as Lawren Harris and Alex Colville, then married fellow artist Christopher Pratt and settled down in semi-rural Salmonier, Newfoundland. Hers has been a long and notable career.

What sets Pratt's work apart is the manner in which she uses photographs from life as the model for her paintings. She claims that the camera allows her to capture those magical moments of intense perceptual delight, a luminosity that gives her work a decided sexual charge.

The Beaverbrook Art Gallery and its curator, Tom Smart, are the creators of both this book and the acclaimed exhibition of the same name. Beautifully produced and brilliantly illustrated, the book is complemented by Smart's biographical and critical text.

Photorealism of this order is not to everyone's taste, which probably only goes to show that one person's sexual charge is another person's Emmenthal.

Zastrozzi, The Master of Discipline: A Melodrama (1977)

GEORGE F. WALKER

Born and raised in Toronto's East End, George Walker was driving a cab and had seen only one play when he responded to Factory Theatre Lab's poster seeking new playwrights. Soon after, he became the Lab's playwright-in-residence and went on to dominate English-language theatre in Canada, winning numerous honours including the Chalmers, the Dora Mavor Moore and the Governor General's Literary Award.

Inspired by reading a description of Percy Bysshe Shelley's novel of the same name, Walker's play pits the European master-criminal Zastrozzi against his idealistic opposite, Verezzi, in a darkly comic confrontation between good and evil. The work is a strange and powerful combination of old-fashioned Gothic melodrama and intellectual sophistication.

With over a hundred productions, including a number of international successes, *Zastrozzi* is one of the most critically acclaimed works by, arguably, Canada's most successful anglophone playwright.

The Valour and the Horror:
The Untold Story of Canadians in
the Second World War (1991)

MERRILY WEISBORD AND MERILYN SIMONDS MOHR

This is the book version of the hugely controversial and stimulating television series of the same name by brothers Brian
and Terence McKenna. The text relies heavily on their research
and as such is open to the same criticisms as those levelled
against the TV series. The complaints came from many quarters:
historians, journalists and politicians (triggering a Senate inquiry).
Veterans felt that their efforts during the war were diminished
by the series' accusations of brutality, incompetence and, in
some cases, cowardice.

The McKennas claim that for every critic there is a supporter,
and that even their most vociferous opponents support many
of their main points. History, they say, is a matter of interpretation,
and it is important to present as full an account as possible: "The
country must know war in its fullness. Let us celebrate the valour.
But let us speak the evil and the horror. People will be torn
by these two things. But let them know what war is really about."

In presenting an unorthodox viewpoint, the book and the
TV series promote valuable debate on important issues and beliefs.
At the same time, the use of personal reminiscences provides
an authentic impression of the experiences of Canadians who
were actually fighting, and dying, in Europe and Asia.

SOME

TREASURES

"We live in an empty place

filled with wonders."

writer Peter C. Newman, *Maclean's*, October 1973

Encyclopedia of Canadian Cuisine (1963)

L'encyclopédie de la cuisine canadienne (French original, 1963)

JEHANE BENOÎT

Is Canada still the country where "everything is cooked in maple sugar"? Hardly. In 1964, however, the editors of Madame Jehane Benoît's *Encyclopedia of Canadian Cuisine* thought this world view of Canadian cuisine worthy of mention. The willingness to embrace the traditions of many cultures, both in our society and in our cooking pots, has often left Canadians and non-Canadians with no clear sense of this country's culinary uniqueness. Madame Benoît introduced Canadian cuisine to Canadians, proving that we could deliciously combine the cooking traditions of other countries into one that was distinctly our own. At the same time, she helped to raise our international profile above the level of maple sugar and tourtière.

Like the *Joy of Cooking*, the best-selling *Encyclopedia of Canadian Cuisine* is a cookbook for all occasions. Recipes for intricate dishes and wine making appear alongside basic directions for boiling meat, and advice on the number and type of dinner plates a bride needs for her dining-room trousseau.

Today, Canadian chefs, cookbooks and television cooking shows abound. We may no longer believe that "A woman's culture and taste are reflected . . . in the way she sets up her kitchen," but it is in part due to Jehane Benoît and her encyclopedia that Canadian cuisine has achieved its present popularity. The tourtière recipe isn't bad, either.

The Sacred Tree: Reflections on Native American Spirituality (1989)

JUDIE BOPP, MICHAEL BOPP, LEE BROWN AND PHIL LANE
ILLUSTRATED BY PATRICIA LUCAS

Forty Native elders and community leaders met in Lethbridge, Alberta, in December 1982, to seek ways to save their communities from the destructive forces of alcoholism, drug abuse and poverty. They shared a vision: to restore health to their people by placing Native spirituality and cultural knowledge into the public school curriculum.

This book is a product of that vision. The sacred tree symbolizes the ancient spiritual teachings of the elders, through which one attains protection, nourishment, growth and wholeness. The richly illustrated text leads the reader on a journey of self-discovery, travelling around the medicine wheel. The journey begins in the East, the place of sunrise, infancy and springtime; this is a period of innocence, spontaneity, hope and trust. The South is noonday, youthfulness and summer; it is the time for physical vigour, determination, loyalty, love and generosity. The West represents afternoon, adulthood and autumn; its lessons are self-acceptance, reflection, humility and sacrifice for the good of all. The North is sunset, old age and winter; this is the time for insight, completion, the attainment of goals and freedom from fear. Altogether, the medicine wheel describes a life fully experienced.

The Sacred Tree demonstrates how indigenous images and ethics can be used to enrich individuals and communities. Accompanied by a teacher's guide, videos and other learning aids, the book is being used in schools across Canada and the United States.

The Incredible Journey (1960)

SHEILA BURNFORD

Sheila Burnford's gripping tale of survival is set in the beautiful, severe wilderness of northern Ontario. Three animals—a young Labrador retriever, an old pit bull terrier and a Siamese cat—have been left with a friend while their owners are away in Europe. The three decide to make their way home, and so begins a 400-km (250-mile) trek through the rugged Canadian Shield. On the journey, they face down starvation, harsh elements, encounters with bad-tempered bobcats and bears, and run-ins with well-meaning humans who try to detain them. In the end, the animals triumph by combining their very different skills, sharing their limited food and looking after one another. The reunion with their owners is joyful and moving.

The Incredible Journey is high drama: unsentimental, authentic, yet heartwarming. Burnford writes from intimate knowledge of the North, to which she emigrated from Scotland in 1951. The animals are modelled after her own pets: each has a vivid, believable personality. The writing is spare, a story of courage and devotion that is simply and lovingly told.

The novel is very popular: it has been translated into sixteen languages and adapted to film several times. The recipient of numerous literary awards, the book is truly a Canadian classic.

The Emily Carr Omnibus (1993)

The Complete Writings of Emily Carr (paperback edition, 1997)

Emily Carr

Emily Carr is now recognized as a remarkable writer whose short stories, diaries and reminiscences rival the beauty of her paintings. As with her art, she worked hard to hone her words into stark, simple images that eliminate vagueness or clutter in favour of precision and impact. This omnibus includes all seven of her published works.

The short stories in *The Book of Small* record Carr's childhood memories of small-town life in 1870s Victoria, British Columbia. *Growing Pains* sketches her family life through to art schools in San Francisco, England and France, where she first encountered modern art movements. *Pause* presents her acute and funny observation of patients, staff and visitors at the English sanatorium where she spent eighteen months recovering from exhaustion. The best known of her books is *Klee Wyck* (it means "Laughing One," the aboriginal name she was given), which details her travels along the West Coast, making contact with Native people and painting forests and the remnants of ancient village sites. This period is also documented in *Hundreds and Thousands*, the diary of her thoughts about painting and daily life, her meeting with the artists of the Group of Seven, and her experiences in old age.

Carr's direct and humorous writings have always appealed equally to ordinary readers and to cultural experts. Her writing is today being applied to feminist, First Nations and environmental studies.

Son of Raven, Son of Deer:
Fables of the Tse-shaht People (1967)

GEORGE CLUTESI

Europeans have recorded aboriginal folk tales since colonization began in Canada, but it was not until 1967 that a First
Nations author set down his own tribal stories. George Clutesi,
a renowned actor, artist and chief of the Vancouver Island Tse-
shaht people, intended these tales for Native children as well as
for "the more reasoning of the non-Indian." The book was an
immediate success and was adopted as a text for schools in British
Columbia, another important first for aboriginal authors.

Son of Raven, Son of Deer presents twelve stories enlivened by
short verses and Clutesi's own drawings. The main characters are
Ko-ishin-mit, a greedy and boastful raven, and Au-tush-mit, a
happy but sometimes foolish deer. The tales reveal how humans
first gained fire, encounters with the shadow people, the perils
of fishing for herring, why Deer has long ears and Raven is burned
black, and how a person becomes a true champion or a poor sport.

Told with charm and gentle humour, Clutesi's stories convey
a great deal of wisdom about respect for the earth, civility toward
others and being true to oneself. More than thirty years after
publication, this small book still delights and instructs.

The Deptford Trilogy

Fifth Business: A Novel (1970)
The Manticore: A Novel (1972)
World of Wonders (1975)

ROBERTSON DAVIES

Circuses, child abuse, the veneration of saints, magic, Jungian psychology—Robertson Davies serves up a heady literary brew, dense with symbols but always elegant and humorous. The novelist was in his mid-fifties when he started on this three-some, and the maturity shows.

A snowball fight is the pivotal event out of which all else grows. Percy Boy Staunton packs a rock inside the snowball he aims at Dunstan Ramsey. But it strikes a very pregnant Mrs. Dempster on the head, leading to the premature birth of Paul and the permanent hospitalization of the mother. Each of these three male characters in turn becomes the central focus of the ongoing story: Ramsey in *Fifth Business*, Staunton in *The Manticore* and Dempster in *World of Wonders*. The trilogy has been likened to the three panels of an altar: on a symbolic level, life's characters are shown to be good, evil or simply terribly confused.

Davies's novels are examples of that altogether rare breed: intelligent, gripping stories, written in high literary style with great comedic panache. His achievement stands at the high point of Canada's literary history.

Dictionary of Canadian Biography (1966–)

Volume I: GEORGE W. BROWN, GENERAL EDITOR
Volume II: DAVID M. HAYNE, GENERAL EDITOR
Volumes III to XII: GEORGE W. BROWN, DAVID M. HAYNE
AND FRANCESS G. HALPENNY, GENERAL EDITORS
Volume XII and XIV: RAMSAY COOK, GENERAL EDITOR

This monumental undertaking—a national treasure—has now reached fourteen volumes and is still growing. Each book contains three hundred to six hundred alphabetically arranged articles on Canadians who have in some way distinguished themselves. It is a gold mine of unique and valuable information, dates, places and events.

Volume I covers a considerable stretch of time, from the year 1000 to 1700 A.D. Entries range from Abraham, John (a scoundrel who in 1681 absconded with his salary advance, rose to become governor of Port Nelson, and ended his days pirating on the St. Lawrence River)—to Zeno, Nicolo and Antonio (family history claims these Venetian brothers sailed the north Atlantic in 1380 and buried treasure in Nova Scotia, though the story is here labelled a crude fabrication). Subsequent volumes have been published every few years, each covering a ten- to forty-year period. The most recent volume brings the series up to 1920.

The *Dictionary of Canadian Biography* is an indispensable aid to historical researchers, but it is equally a compulsive and fascinating read for browsers. Here are the powerful, the obscure, the conniving, the saintly, even the criminally insane, each set against the background of his or her times—Canadians all, and proof that we are not nearly so dull as some might think.

The Wind Has Wings:
Poems from Canada (1968)

The New Wind Has Wings: Poems from Canada
(2nd edition, 1984)

Mary Alice Downie and
Barbara Robertson, compilers
illustrated by Elizabeth Cleaver

Until this remarkable anthology, volumes of Canadian poetry
for children looked like dismal textbooks. What a welcome
innovation this book was: a riot of dazzling colour with bouncing,
joyful text that expands upon young children's natural pleasure
in the nursery rhyme. The editors, travelling across Canada's
vast literary landscape, located seventy-seven delicious poems
by forty-eight poets. The book's universally enthusiastic reception
resulted in a second edition in 1984 that deletes only two but
adds fifteen more verses.

Traditional folk songs from French, English, Yiddish and
Inuktitut are interspersed with rousing, rhyming storytelling
poems ("The Shooting of Dan McGrew"); poems that view the
world through an animal's eyes ("How and When and Where and
Why"); poems about the supernatural world of myth and magic
("The Spider Danced a Cosy Jig"); and of course, verses by many
of our best-known modern poets (Raymond Souster's swooping
"Flight of the Roller Coaster").

Illustrated with bold images based on shadow puppets,
paper cuts and woodblock prints, this popular book heralded a
new direction in truly beautiful Canadian books for children.
Thirty years later, it still enthralls kids and adults.

The Game: A Thoughtful and Provocative Look at a Life in Hockey (1983)

Ken Dryden

Hockey holds a special place in Canadian life. Whether you follow the game or not, it is a symbol of our national identity, with the power to ignite passions and patriotism that are sparked by little else.

Much has been written about "our" game, but few authors have captured its essence as forcefully as Ken Dryden. His perspective is unique: as an outstanding goaltender with the legendary Montréal Canadiens for eight exceptional seasons, he knows the world of hockey inside out. And as a lawyer used to working with words, he draws the reader into that world with a literary skill and intelligence seldom seen in sports writing.

The book is a diary of nine days in the 1978–79 season, Dryden's last as a player, and a moment of transition that leads to these incisive reflections. Along with the story of his own child-hood apprenticeship for hockey stardom, he offers sketches of famous teammates and coaches, a history of changes that made the sport more scientific and less brutal, and analyses of plays on the ice and in the locker room. But the special strength of this book is his meditations on the game: the privileges that come with celebrity, the extravagant salaries, the violence, the on-ice atmosphere of excitement, crisis and heightened immediacy.

These are sensations that only a player can describe, brought to life in one of the best books ever written about the sport. You will never again watch a hockey game in quite the same way.

Sally Go Round the Sun:
300 Songs, Rhymes and Games of
Canadian Children (1969)

EDITH FOWKE, COMPILER AND EDITOR
KEITH MacMILLAN, MUSICAL ARRANGER
ILLUSTRATED BY CARLOS MARCHIORI

> Sally go round the sun,
> Sally go round the moon,
> Sally go round the chimney top
> Every afternoon!

Children take delight in the rhythms, music and imagery of language. This energetic and joyous collection of rhymes and songs recorded by folklorist Edith Fowke is a national treasure. Skipping chants, clapping and singing games, ball bounces, foot and finger plays, nonsense, counting rhymes, taunts and teases, and silly songs—these exuberant moments from the subculture of childhood were gathered mainly in Ontario during the early 1960s. Careful notes detail dates and places as well as how to play the singing games.

Passed down orally from older to younger child without ever the need for an adult go-between, the folklore within these covers can be enjoyed by readers of any age; parents and teachers are tendered a special invitation.

Honoured in 1970 as an outstanding Canadian children's book, *Sally Go Round the Sun* is also a marvel of witty and inventive graphic design that this celebration of childhood deserves.

The Great Code:
The Bible and Literature (1982)

Words with Power: Being a Second Study of the Bible and Literature (1990)

NORTHROP FRYE

These two books, among the most important surveys of myth and religion ever written, are Northrop Frye's landmark achievements.

According to Frye in *The Great Code*, the Bible is not primarily a history nor an anthology of poems, myths and narratives. Rather, it is a unity. Later stories recall, elaborate on, or are foreshadowed by earlier ones (the twelve apostles, for example, echo the twelve tribes of Israel). The Bible is many stories that collectively tell one progressive story of quest and salvation: how humanity lost an earthly paradise, struggles to live in the present world and may yet recover harmony.

Words with Power expands this idea to embrace the whole of Western literature. Frye believes that our literary heritage is a unified body of work bound by its origins in the Bible. These stories—the lost paradise, the heroic quest, the garden and the city, liberation from bondage, the rise of the lowly and the humbling of the great—appear again and again, spreading out from the Bible into fairy tales, epic poems, soap operas and comic books. One work connects with all the others, and the reader can follow its thread back to the original religious experience.

Frye's work has massively influenced modern theology, education and critical studies. Not an easy read, his books are accessible to any reader with some intellectual stamina and a good dictionary.

The Selected Stories of
Mavis Gallant (1996)

Mavis Gallant

Mavis Gallant's short stories are deeply informed by the dis-
locations of her own past. When the author's father died in
the 1930s, her Protestant mother placed her in a Catholic school in
Québec and left the country to remarry. Later, the objectivity that
Gallant practised as a journalist helped to hone her observant eye
and matter-of-fact narrative voice. Permanent relocation to Paris
in 1950 situated her in a world of impoverished post-war refugees.

Gallant writes about the transient, the displaced, the escapee
from provincial backwaters, the émigré, the unnoticed and fright-
ened child. Her self-deluded characters yearn for security, even
as they move restlessly from one unsatisfying, temporary home to
another. They seem deliberately forgetful of their pasts and dis-
trustful of the shifting present. They get by, uneasily, finding
small comforts on the margins of an uncertain world. Gallant's
portraits are subtle, both tolerant and unforgiving.

Selected Stories presents fifty-two of Gallant's best short
fictions, written over half a century and drawn from eight collections. She is widely regarded as being among the finest short-story
writers in the English language.

A River Never Sleeps (1946)

RODERICK L. HAIG-BROWN

Two years of working in Vancouver Island logging camps convinced the young Englishman Roderick Haig-Brown to permanently emigrate to Canada in 1931. His first book appeared that same year, launching a writing career that spanned sixty-five years and thirty-two books. He is arguably Canada's most poetic advocate for wilderness conservation.

A River Never Sleeps is a lyrical classic on the art of fly-fishing, a loving recollection of twenty years spent on the rivers of England and western Canada. Haig-Brown describes the young angler refining his skills, the lore and ethics of the sport, the ardent joy of immersion in the wilderness. The book is a meditation on the mystical interconnectedness of forest and water, as well as the humans and other life that depend upon them.

Painting in Canada:
A History (1966, 2nd edition 1977)

J. Russell Harper

This landmark book on three hundred years of painting in Canada offers a comprehensive survey that has yet to be surpassed. Russell Harper's aim was "to write a history that presents for the general public an accurate, documented survey of Canada's very considerable aesthetic achievement in painting, one that also incorporates the scholarship and research that has been done on the subject to date." In a clear, strong narrative voice, he did.

The original edition of *Painting in Canada* was a project to celebrate Canada's centennial in 1967. The book was welcomed by critics for the high quality of its scholarship and for filling a gap in Canada's cultural history.

In 1977, a concise second edition appeared, revised and updated, but not brought up to date (still ending with the 1950s). Unlike the lavishly illustrated original, the second edition had only a small section of black-and-white reproductions. A Canadian art survey of the original calibre, bringing the history up to the present, is sorely needed.

The author of several books on Canadian art, Harper was curator of Canadian art at the National Gallery of Canada, and chief curator of the McCord Museum at McGill University.

Portrait of a Period: A Collection of Notman Photographs, 1856 to 1915 (1967)

J. Russell Harper and Stanley Triggs, editors

William Notman came to Canada from Scotland in 1856. Over the next half century, he and his sons created one of the most fascinating photographic records of late nineteenth- and early twentieth-century life in this country. In Canada's centennial year (1967), more than two hundred of these superb glass-plate photographs, chosen from the collection of some four hundred thousand plates at the McCord Museum at McGill University, were reproduced in this impressive coffee-table book. The photographs are divided into themes of people, cities, sea and countryside.

Here we see a young John A. Macdonald as he appeared in 1863, there the famous portrait of Sitting Bull from 1886. Panoramic views of the country's flourishing young cities include Calgary, Vancouver and Victoria. There is a wealth of period detail to savour in pictures of a crew aboard an east-coast fishing schooner, a cook shanty on the Ottawa River or a meeting of the Northwest Council.

Notman's photographs were recognized in their time for their superior quality. Today, they are among the finest images of Canadian life in the time shortly after Confederation.

Northwest Coast Indian Art:
An Analysis of Form (1965)

BILL HOLM

The look of Northwest Coast Native art — distinctive, stylized creatures and graceful yet bold formlines — is known and appreciated around the world. Major pieces such as totem poles, murals and bronze sculptures are on view in public places as well as in museums and galleries. Yet very few people understand the meaning behind the designs.

In 1965, when artist, art historian, professor, curator and author Bill Holm published *Northwest Coast Indian Art*, he provided a vocabulary for describing this art and a system for understanding its design elements. He based his work on the close study of four hundred objects (including jewelry, boxes, screens, panels, dishes, coffin fronts and masks). Using photos and his own illustrations, Holm points out the significance of the colours used, the relationships between positive and negative space, the arrangement of body parts and more abstract shapes, and the use of the black formlines that surround and define design units.

Holm is not writing for casual readers, but this is an essential work for those who want to learn about the art of the First Nations of the Northwest Coast.

Encyclopedia of Music in Canada
(1981, 2nd edition 1992)

Helmut Kallman, Gilles Potvin and
Kenneth Winters, editors

In 1969, Floyd Chalmers, then chairman of the Maclean-
Hunter publishing group, was dismayed to discover how very
little had been published on the subject of music in Canada.
He gathered a group of musicians, scholars and business people,
who after twelve years produced this indispensable record of
three centuries of music making.

From Hank Snow, the famous country-music songwriter
born in Nova Scotia, to Anne Murray's hit song "Snowbird," the
monumental encyclopedia is opinionated, compulsively readable and full of surprises.

The enlarged second edition of 1992 includes some 3,700
articles that cover the range of music: rock, pop, jazz, folk, big
band, rap, classical, Native, religious and New Age. Here are histories of particular songs; biographies of musicians, composers,
singers, teachers, conductors and choruses; even articles on individual cities, musical instruments and record companies. Also
included are bibliographies and discographies. Five hundred
photographs illustrate people, places, scores, concert programs
and sheet music.

Alligator Pie (1974)

DENNIS LEE
ILLUSTRATED BY FRANK NEWFELD

> Alligator pie, alligator pie,
> If I don't get some I think I'm gonna die.

So begins the rebellious chant that heralded a new and lively age in Canadian poetry for children. Dennis Lee's verse speaks to children on their own terms, using a patchwork of hockey sticks, skyscrapers, Ookpiks and strange place names (with which our country is replete) like Kamloops, Moose Jaw and Chicoutimi. The result is a fun-filled, jumbled collage that parallels the Canadian mosaic from a child's point of view.

Lee, a Governor General's Literary Award–winning poet for adults, was dismayed when he realized that the traditional rhymes he recited to his young children were filled with foreign references. *Alligator Pie* is his remedy—a new folklore, composed of images and ideas relevant to Canadian kids. Granted that alligators, elephants and especially itchy monkeys are not native to Canada—but they do exist in the imaginations of all children. And when an itchy monkey is caught on Yonge Street, or a hockey stick is traded for alligator stew, the result is poetry that is fun to read and undeniably Canadian.

Imagining Canadian Literature: The Selected Letters of Jack McClelland (1998)

Jack McClelland
Sam Solecki, editor

A profound and permanent change in Canada's literary landscape began in 1952, when Jack McClelland took control of
the stolid publishing firm of McClelland and Stewart. Instead
of acting mainly as a distributor for British and American books,
he began to publish emerging Canadian authors—then unknown
names like Pierre Berton, Al Purdy, Irving Layton, Peter Newman,
Leonard Cohen, Marian Engel, Brian Moore, Gabrielle Roy,
Hugh Hood and Michael Ondaatje.

McClelland knew how to get headlines, and over time he
created a wide audience for Canadian poetry and fiction. His pioneering faith in our literature made possible the extraordinary
early 1970s flowering of small and regional Canadian presses that
published hundreds of talented new writers.

This collection of McClelland's letters illustrates his firm
belief: "publish authors, not books." Written to and from the icons
of Canadian literature, the letters document three decades in
the career of a flamboyant literary nationalist. He supports,
cajoles, threatens and parties with these often fragile creative egos.
He battles financial crises and the forces of censorship; trades
insults with Mordecai Richler and Farley Mowat; encourages
Margaret Laurence; respects Margaret Atwood; chews out Earle
Birney. They bounce back with complaints, outrageous demands,
blind rage, and often hilarious and finely crafted barbs—as
well as some respect and thanks.

Nowhere in Canadian publishing is there a more immediate
and lively reflection of our literature's coming of age.

Anne of Green Gables (1908)

Lucy Maud Montgomery

In 1908, an original and distinctly Canadian heroine appeared in children's literature: Anne Shirley, with her carrot-red hair and freckles, extravagant vocabulary and boundless enthusiasm, was destined to become an international star.

The orphaned Anne arrives at Green Gables by mistake — Matthew and Marilla Cuthbert had requested a boy for adoption, to help out on the farm. But Anne, whose romantic imagination transforms rural Prince Edward Island into a world of beauty and possibility, ultimately enchants them. Through the trials and mischief of growing up, whether accidentally dyeing her hair green or getting her best friend drunk on raspberry cordial (unaware of its alcoholic content), Anne's determination to create a joyful world captivates readers, as surely as it did Matthew and Marilla.

Lucy Maud Montgomery shows a real understanding of children, what angers or amuses them, and how astutely they assess the adult world. While the success of *Anne of Green Gables* encouraged her to write seven sequels, Montgomery probably did not imagine that her character would become a national icon. The story has been made into a musical and more than one movie, and the fictional Green Gables is now a tourist attraction, luring thousands of visitors to Prince Edward Island every year in search of Anne's magic.

Jacob Two-Two Meets the Hooded Fang (1975)

MORDECAI RICHLER

ILLUSTRATED BY FRITZ WEGNER

In his triumphant first novel for children, novelist Mordecai Richler provides a satirical view of how children view adult society. It began as a bedtime story that Richler told to his youngest child, Jacob, and grew from there.

In the book, Jacob is two plus two plus two years old. In a fantastic dream, he believes he has been sentenced to Slimers' Isle, a children's prison, for committing the greatest of crimes: insulting an adult. Children are attracted by the comic appeal of the ridiculous adults, from Louis Loser to Mistress Fowl and Master Fish, to the Hooded Fang himself. This is a traditional tale of good versus evil. Richler demonstrates that children are far from helpless and can, with a little teamwork, overcome even the most difficult circumstances.

The award-winning *Jacob Two-Two Meets the Hooded Fang* was translated into several languages and adapted as a musical as well as a film. Richler wrote two delightful sequels: *Jacob Two-Two and the Dinosaur* (1987) and *Jacob Two-Two's First Spy Case* (1995).

5BX Plan for Physical Fitness (1958)

Royal Canadian Air Force

The next time you attempt twenty push-ups, consider this: your red face may well be the warm flush of national pride. Decades before fitness became trendy, this small Canadian volume was a best-seller, and its health program was used by civilians and soldiers around the world. Knowingly or not, pretty much everyone in Canada has been exposed to at least one of the exercises in the book.

The "five basic exercises" (hence the title 5BX) are toe touches, head rises, leg rises, push-ups and running on the spot, combined to benefit the major muscle groups, heart and lungs. Concerned about the low level of fitness of its personnel, the Royal Canadian Air Force decided it needed a simple exercise plan that could be followed anywhere without complex equipment. The program was devised by Dr. William Orban, a football player, sports coach and runner. Orban's program is simple and snappy, allowing an individual's fitness level to improve slowly. Part of the plan's popularity is due to the fact that it can be learned easily and completed in just eleven minutes a day.

At the time of its publication, the 5BX book filled an information void. Awareness of the benefits of exercise was new, and the 5BX, with its adaptability and promise of fitness without pain, was instantly popular. A women's version, the XBX, was published in the early 1960s. By 1981 there were 15 million copies of 5BX in print, including a dozen translations into European and Asian languages. It is the forerunner of the fitness books that crowd bookstore and library shelves today.

Great Scott!: The Best of Jay Scott's Movie Reviews (1994)

Jay Scott

Jay Scott was one of Canada's most provocative and insightful film critics, best known as a reviewer for the *Globe and Mail* and various national magazines, as well as the host of educational television programs about film.

Bucking the trend of indulging in Hollywood press junkets and cranking out reviews as promotional pap, Scott wrote columns (125 are collected here) that are brave, thoughtful, funny, even sometimes outrageous critiques of what he saw as the best and worst the medium offered. He was a master stylist, and his writing still makes for enjoyable reading. Scott could jab with wicked one-liners: his comment on *The Shining* was that "Kubrick certainly doesn't fail small." However, his reviews were more notable for the thoughtful way they pointed out links from one particular film to other films, as well as to related works of literature, art or even fashion.

Whether championing a little-known Canadian director or skewering a famous foreign filmmaker, Scott presented his insights knowledgeably and delectably.

The Best of Robert Service (1953)

ROBERT SERVICE

> There are strange things done in the midnight sun
> By the men who moil for gold;
> The Arctic trails have their secret tales
> That would make your blood run cold;

So begins "The Cremation of Sam McGee," one of Robert Service's best-loved and most-memorized poems, a bizarrely comic and very catchy account of a gold miner from Tennessee whose corpse expresses warm appreciation for a toasty funeral. The equally famous "The Shooting of Dan McGrew," as well as many other lively works, are gathered together in *The Best of Robert Service*.

Born in England, Service spent several years in the Yukon, where he was inspired by the rugged landscape and the even more rugged people who lived and worked there. He writes about the gold rush days—about the miners, trappers and outlaws in search of fortune and fame. Full of the sounds and rhythms of those colourful times, his poems are rhyming verses in a folksy style.

Service made a significant contribution to the literature of the Canadian North; his haunting, vigorous verse brought that strange world to an international audience. This collection is a wonderful introduction to a writer often dubbed "the poet of the Yukon" and sometimes "Canada's Kipling."

The Stone Diaries (1993)

Carol Shields

Within two years of publication, this superb novel was nominated for Britain's prestigious Booker Prize, won the Governor General's Literary Award for fiction, and, in the United States, received both the Pulitzer Prize and the National Book Critics Award—all this for a straightforward telling of the life of a truly unremarkable woman.

The novel is structured as a biography of the very ordinary Daisy Goodwill, a wife and mother who, late in life, begins an uncharacteristic review of her past. Her story leaps forward as a series of episodes that span the century. Daisy's life is one of small disappointments, aches and ailments, everyday resignation to domestic toil and family duty, and hopeful attempts to make things *nice*. She is the unreliable narrator of a life defined by others, filled with details that never quite come into meaningful focus. Her active but unfulfilled mind has slowly turned to stone under the weight of immense, unexpressed unhappiness.

Carol Shield's handling of this material is lucid and elegant, her tale filled with gripping moments, vivid characters and meticulous details that build stunning word pictures. Like Daisy, the reader is compelled to explore the nature of biography, the meaning that underlies events and, finally, the essential mystery of human life.

Dance Canada:
An Illustrated History (1989)

Max Wyman

This fine example of a coffee-table book offers a dramatic collection of the kind of gorgeous photography often associated with dance. The text is clear and knowledgeable, with something of the critic's incisive insight. There is light coverage of dance in the colonial period, but the story of dance in Canada is very much of the twentieth century and, more particularly, of the post-war years when it took root. And what a story it is. The histories of the nation's great ballet and modern dance companies are all here—the Royal Winnipeg Ballet, the National Ballet, Les Grands Ballets Canadiens and many more—rising and falling, driven by individual temperament, intercompany rivalry and grand ambition.

Max Wyman, an arts columnist and dance critic, set out to describe the creative context from which Canada's leading dancers and dance companies emerged. Keenly aware that he is dealing with the beginning of a tradition, not its crowning glory, his knowledgeable telling is notable for its affectionate but unsentimental presentation.

Afterword

It is always wonderful for a library director to see meaningful and exciting projects emerge spontaneously from the library staff. *Great Canadian Books of the Century* has been such a project, and seeing the end result is truly rewarding. To all the staff who contributed time and energy to nurture this from idea to finished product, my thanks and appreciation. To all those who supported us with ideas, funding and other assistance — we couldn't have done it without you. Particularly the publisher, Scott McIntyre, who came to lunch with Cheryl Ryll and me, and by the end of our time together, announced "I'm in!", and Kyle Mitchell, former chair of the Vancouver Public Library Board — we are most grateful for your help.

I hope that you, the reader, have found this book to be as challenging, enjoyable and even frustrating, as I have. The pleasure of being reminded of books read many years ago was balanced for me with the mild indignation at missing authors and titles that, in my opinion, should have been included (for example, Eric Nicol's humour, Phyllis Webb's poetry and *Chin Chiang and the Dragon's Dance* by Ian Wallace). If you had the same reactions, then we have succeeded.

Finally, special thanks to Cheryl Ryll and Anne Stockdale, for making this not just a job but a labour of love. And to all those who contributed in any way to this project, our sincere thanks. The good things, we owe to you; any errors are, as always, ours.

MADELEINE AALTO

DIRECTOR,

VANCOUVER PUBLIC LIBRARY

Bibliography

Acorn, Milton. *I've Tasted My Blood: Poems, 1956 to 1968*. Selected by Al Purdy. Toronto: Ryerson Press, 1969.

Adachi, Ken. *The Enemy That Never Was: [A History of the Japanese Canadians]*. Generations: A History of Canada's Peoples. Toronto: McClelland and Stewart, 1976.

Allan, Ted, and Sydney Gordon. *The Scalpel, the Sword: The Story of Dr. Norman Bethune*. Boston: Little, Brown; Toronto: McClelland and Stewart, 1952.

Assembly of First Nations. *Breaking the Silence: An Interpretive Study of Residential School Impact and Healing as Illustrated by the Stories of First Nations Individuals*. Ottawa: [First Nations Health Commission], 1994.

Atwood, Margaret. *The Edible Woman*. Toronto: McClelland and Stewart, 1969.

Atwood, Margaret. *The Journals of Susanna Moodie: Poems*. Toronto: Oxford University Press, 1970.

Bantock, Nick. *The Golden Mean: In Which the Extraordinary Correspondence of Griffin & Sabine Concludes*. Vancouver: Raincoast Books, 1993.

Bantock, Nick. *Griffin & Sabine: An Extraordinary Correspondence*. Vancouver: Raincoast Books, 1991.

Bantock, Nick. *The Griffin & Sabine Trilogy*. 3 vols. Vancouver: Raincoast Books, 1993.

Bantock, Nick. *Sabine's Notebook: In Which the Extraordinary Correspondence of Griffin & Sabine Continues*. Vancouver: Raincoast Books, 1992.

Benoît, Jehane. *Encyclopedia of Canadian Cuisine*. Montréal: Messageries du Saint-Laurent, 1963.

Benoît, Jehane. *L'encyclopédie de la cuisine canadienne*. Montréal: Messageries du Saint-Laurent, 1963.

Bercuson, David Jay. *Confrontation at Winnipeg: Labour, Industrial Relations, and the General Strike*. Montréal: McGill-Queen's University Press, 1974.

Berton, Pierre. *The Comfortable Pew: A Critical Look at Christianity and the Religious Establishment in the New Age*. Foreword by Ernest Harrison. Toronto: McClelland and Stewart, 1965.

Berton, Pierre. *The National Dream: The Great Railway, 1871–1881*. Toronto: McClelland and Stewart, 1970.

Berton, Pierre. *The Last Spike: The Great Railway, 1881–1885*. Toronto: McClelland and Stewart, 1971.
    Both volumes published together in 1972 under title: *The Impossible Railway: The Building of the Canadian Pacific*. New York: Knopf, 1972.

Birney, Earle. *David and Other Poems*. Toronto: The Ryerson Press, 1942.

Blades, Ann. *Mary of Mile 18*. Montréal: Tundra Books; Plattsburgh, N.Y.: Tundra Books of Northern New York, 1971.

Blais, Marie-Claire. *Une saison dans la vie d'Emmanuel: roman.* Collection les romanciers du jour. Montréal: Éditions du Jour, 1965.

Blais, Marie-Claire. *A Season in the Life of Emmanuel.* Translated by Derek Coltman. Introduction by Edmund Wilson. New York: Farrar, Straus and Giroux; Toronto: Ambassador Books Ltd., 1966.

Bliss, Michael. *The Discovery of Insulin.* Toronto: McClelland and Stewart, 1982. Alternate title in paperback ed.: *Glory Enough for All: The Discovery of Insulin.* Toronto: McClelland and Stewart, 1988.

Bliss, Michael. *Northern Enterprise: Five Centuries of Canadian Business.* Toronto: McClelland and Stewart, 1987.

Bopp, Judie, Michael Bopp, Lee Brown, and Phil Lane, produced collaboratively. *The Sacred Tree: Reflections on Native American Spirituality.* Illustrated by Patricia Lucas. 3rd ed. Twin Lakes, Wis.: Lotus Light Publications, 1989.

Bopp, Judie, Michael Bopp, Lee Brown, and Phil Lane, produced collaboratively. *The Sacred Tree: Reflections on Native American Spirituality.* Lethbridge, Alta.: Four Worlds Development Press, 1984.

Broadfoot, Barry. *Ten Lost Years, 1929–1939: Memories of Canadians Who Survived the Depression.* Toronto: Doubleday Canada; Garden City, N.Y.: Doubleday, 1973.

Brown, Craig, ed. *The Illustrated History of Canada.* 2nd. rev. ed. Toronto: Lester Publishing, 1996.

Brown, Craig, ed. *The Illustrated History of Canada.* Toronto: Lester and Orpen Dennys, 1987.

Burnford, Sheila. *The Incredible Journey.* Illustrated by Carl Burger. Boston: Little, Brown, 1960.

The Canadian Encyclopedia. James H. Marsh, editor-in-chief. 2nd ed. [substantially expanded and updated] 4 vols. Edmonton: Hurtig Publishers, 1988.

The Canadian Encyclopedia. James H. Marsh, editor-in-chief. 3 vols. Edmonton: Hurtig Publishers, 1985.

Cardinal, Harold. *The Unjust Society: The Tragedy of Canada's Indians.* Edmonton: M. G. Hurtig, 1969.

Carr, Emily. *The Emily Carr Omnibus.* Introduction by Doris Shadbolt. Vancouver, Toronto: Douglas and McIntyre, 1993. 1st pbk. ed. issued under title: *The Complete Writings of Emily Carr.* Vancouver, Toronto: Douglas and McIntyre, 1997.

Carrier, Roch. "Le chandail de hockey." In *Les enfants du bonhomme dans la lune.* Montréal: Éditions internationales Alain Stanké lteé, 1979.

Carrier, Roch. *Le chandail de hockey.* Illustrated by Sheldon Cohen. 1st ed. Montréal: Livres Toundra, 1984.

Carrier, Roch. "The Hockey Sweater." In *The Hockey Sweater and Other Stories.* Translated by Sheila Fischman. Toronto: Anansi, 1979.

Carrier, Roch. *The Hockey Sweater.* Translated by Sheila Fischman. Illustrated by Sheldon Cohen. Montréal: Tundra Books, 1984.

Chilton, David Barr. *The Wealthy Barber: The Common Sense Guide to Successful Financial Planning*. Toronto: Stoddart, 1989.

Chilton, David Barr. *The Wealthy Barber: The Common Sense Guide to Successful Financial Planning*. Kitchener, Ont.: Financial Awareness Corporation, 1989.

Clutesi, George. *Son of Raven, Son of Deer: Fables of the Tse-shaht People*. Sidney, B.C.: Gray's, 1967.

Cohen, Leonard. *Stranger Music: Selected Poems and Songs*. Toronto: McClelland and Stewart, 1993.

Collins, Anne. *In the Sleep Room: The Story of the CIA Brainwashing Experiments in Canada*. Toronto: Lester and Orpen Dennys, 1988.

Cott, Jonathan. *Conversations with Glenn Gould*. Boston, Toronto: Little, Brown, 1984.

Craven, Margaret. *I Heard the Owl Call My Name*. Toronto, Vancouver: Clarke, Irwin, 1967.

Davidson, Robert. *Eagle Transforming: The Art of Robert Davidson*. Photographs by Ulli Steltzer. [Introduction by Aldona Jonaitis.] Vancouver, Toronto: Douglas and McIntyre; Seattle: University of Washington Press, 1994.

Davies, Robertson. *The Deptford Trilogy: Fifth Business, The Manticore, World of Wonders*. New York: Viking Penguin, 1983.

Davies, Robertson. *Fifth Business: A Novel*. Toronto: Macmillan of Canada, 1970.

Davies, Robertson. *The Manticore: A Novel*. Toronto: Macmillan of Canada, 1972.

Davies, Robertson. *World of Wonders*. Toronto: Macmillan of Canada, 1975.

de la Roche, Mazo. *Jalna*. Toronto: Macmillan Co. of Canada, 1927.

Dictionary of Canadian Biography. 14 vols. to date. Volume I, George W. Brown, general editor; Volume II, David M. Hayne, general editor; Volumes III to XII, George W. Brown, David M. Hayne and Francess G. Halpenny, general editors; Volumes XIII and XIV, Ramsay Cook, general editor. Toronto: University of Toronto Press, 1966–.

Downie, Mary Alice, and Barbara Robertson, comps. *The New Wind Has Wings: Poems from Canada*. Illustrated by Elizabeth Cleaver. Toronto, Oxford: Oxford University Press, 1984.

Downie, Mary Alice, and Barbara Robertson, comps. *The Wind Has Wings: Poems from Canada*. Illustrated by Elizabeth Cleaver. Toronto: Oxford University Press, 1968.

Doyle, Brian. *Up to Low*. Vancouver, Toronto: Douglas and McIntyre, Groundwood Books, 1982.

Dryden, Ken. *The Game: A Thoughtful and Provocative Look at a Life in Hockey*. Toronto: Macmillan of Canada, 1983.

Ellis, Sarah. *The Baby Project*. Vancouver, Toronto: Douglas and McIntyre, Groundwood Books, 1986.

Encyclopedia of Music in Canada. Helmut Kallmann and Gilles Potvin, eds.; Robin Elliott, and Mark Miller, associate eds. 2nd ed. Toronto, Buffalo, London: University of Toronto Press, 1992.

Encyclopedia of Music in Canada. Helmut Kallmann, Gilles Potvin, and Kenneth Winters, eds. Toronto, Buffalo, London: University of Toronto Press, 1981.

Findley, Timothy. *The Wars*. Toronto: Clarke, Irwin, 1977.

Fowke, Edith, ed. *Folk Songs of Canada*. Richard Johnston, music ed. Illustrated by Elizabeth Wilkes Hoey. Waterloo, Ont.: Waterloo Music Co., 1954.

Fowke, Edith, ed. *More Folk Songs of Canada*. Richard Johnston, music ed. Illustrated by Elizabeth Wilkes Hoey. Waterloo, Ont.: Waterloo Music Co., 1967.

Fowke, Edith, comp. and ed. *Sally Go Round the Sun: [300 Songs, Rhymes, and Games of Canadian Children]*. Musical arrangements by Keith MacMillan. Illustrated by Carlos Marchiori. Toronto: McClelland and Stewart, 1969.

Fraser, Brad. *Unidentified Human Remains and the True Nature of Love*. Winnipeg: Blizzard, 1990.

French, David. *Leaving Home*. Introduction by Urjo Kareda. Toronto: New Press, 1972.

Frye, Northrop. *The Great Code: The Bible and Literature*. Toronto: Academic Press Canada, 1982.

Frye, Northrop. *Words with Power: Being a Second Study of the Bible and Literature*. Markham, Ont.: Viking, 1990.

Gagnon, François-Marc. *Paul-Émile Borduas*. [Montréal]: Montreal Museum of Fine Arts, 1988.

Gagnon, François-Marc. *Paul-Émile Borduas, 1905–1960: biographie critique et analyse de l'oeuvre*. Montréal: Fides, 1978.

Galbraith, John Kenneth. *The Affluent Society*. Boston: Houghton Mifflin, 1958.

Galdikas, Biruté M. F. *Reflections of Eden: My Years with the Orangutans of Borneo*. Boston, Toronto: Little, Brown, 1995.

Gallant, Mavis. *The Selected Stories of Mavis Gallant*. Toronto: McClelland and Stewart, 1996.

Gibson, William. *Neuromancer*. New York: Ace Science Fiction Books, 1984.

Gowans, Alan. *Building Canada: An Architectural History of Canadian Life*. [Rev. and enl. ed. of *Looking at Architecture in Canada* (1958).] Toronto: Oxford University Press, 1966.

Grant, George. *Lament for a Nation: The Defeat of Canadian Nationalism*. Toronto: McClelland and Stewart, 1965.

Gray, John, with Eric Peterson. *Billy Bishop Goes to War: A Play*. Vancouver: Talonbooks, 1981.

Haig-Brown, Roderick L. *Return to the River: A Story of the Chinook Run*. Illustrated by Charles DeFeo. Toronto: Collins, 1941.

Haig-Brown, Roderick L. *A River Never Sleeps*. Illustrated by Louis Darling. Toronto: Collins, 1946.

Harper, J. Russell. *Painting in Canada: A History*. 2nd [concise] ed. [Revised and updated.] Toronto, Buffalo: University of Toronto Press, 1977.

Harper, J. Russell. *Painting in Canada: A History*. Toronto: University of Toronto Press, 1966.

Harper, J. Russell, and Stanley Triggs. *Portrait of a Period: A Collection of Notman Photographs, 1856 to 1915*. Introduction by Edgar Andrew Collard. Montréal: McGill University Press, 1967.

Hébert, Anne. *Kamouraska: A Novel*. Translated by Norman Shapiro. Toronto: Musson Book, 1973.

Hébert, Anne. *Kamouraska: roman*. Paris: Éditions du Seuil, 1970.

Hémon, Louis. *Maria Chapdelaine: A Tale of the Lake St. John Country*. Translated by W. H. Blake. Toronto: Macmillan, 1921.

Hémon, Louis. *Maria Chapdelaine: récit du Canada français*. Montréal: J. A. Lefebvre, 1916. [Originally published in *Le Temps de Paris* (1.–2. 1914)]

Herbert, John. *Fortune and Men's Eyes*. New York: Grove Press, 1967.

Historical Atlas of Canada. Vol. I, *From the Beginning to 1800*. R. Cole Harris, ed., and Geoffrey J. Matthews, cartographer/designer. Toronto, Buffalo, London: University of Toronto Press, 1987.

Historical Atlas of Canada. Vol. II, *The Land Transformed, 1800–1891*. R. Louis Gentilcore, ed., and Geoffrey J. Matthews, cartographer/designer. Toronto, Buffalo, London: University of Toronto Press, 1993.

Historical Atlas of Canada. Vol. III, *Addressing the Twentieth Century, 1891–1961*. Donald Kerr and Deryck W. Holdsworth, eds., and Geoffrey J. Matthews, cartographer/designer. Toronto, Buffalo, London: University of Toronto Press, 1990.

Holm, Bill. *Northwest Coast Indian Art: An Analysis of Form*. Thomas Burke Memorial Washington State Museum. Monograph, no. 1. Seattle: University of Washington Press; Vancouver, Toronto: Douglas and McIntyre, 1965.

Hughes, Monica. *The Keeper of the Isis Light*. London: Hamish Hamilton, 1980.

Innis, Harold A. *The Bias of Communication*. Toronto: University of Toronto Press, 1951.

Innis, Harold A. *The Fur Trade in Canada: An Introduction to Canadian Economic History*. Preface by R. M. MacIver. New Haven: Yale University Press; London: H. Milford, Oxford University Press, 1930.

Jackson, A. Y. *A Painter's Country: The Autobiography of A. Y. Jackson*. Foreword by Vincent Massey. Toronto: Clarke, Irwin, 1958.

Jacobs, Jane. *The Death and Life of Great American Cities*. New York: Random House, 1961.

Karsh, Yousuf. *Portraits of Greatness*. Toronto: University of Toronto Press, 1959.

Kinsella, W. P. *Shoeless Joe*. Boston: Houghton Mifflin, 1982.

Kogawa, Joy. *Obasan*. Toronto: Lester and Orpen Dennys, 1981.

Kusugak, Michael Avaarluk. *Baseball Bats for Christmas*. Illustrated by Vladyana Krykorka. Toronto: Annick Press, 1990.

Laing, G. Blair. *Morrice: A Great Canadian Artist Rediscovered*. Introduction by Jean Sutherland Boggs. Toronto: McClelland and Stewart, 1984.

Laurence, Margaret. *The Diviners*. Toronto: McClelland and Stewart, 1974.

Layton, Irving. *A Wild Peculiar Joy: Selected Poems, 1945–82*. Modern Canadian Poets. Toronto: McClelland and Stewart, 1982.

Leacock, Stephen. *Sunshine Sketches of a Little Town*. Frontispiece by Cyrus Cuneo. London, New York: John Lane, 1912.

Lee, Dennis. *Alligator Pie*. Illustrated by Frank Newfeld. Toronto: Macmillan of Canada, 1974.

Lipsey, Richard G., Paul N. Courant, Douglas D. Purvis and Peter O. Steiner. *Economics*. 10th ed. The HarperCollins Series in Economics. New York: HarperCollins College Publishers, 1993.

Lipsey, Richard G. *Economics*. New York: Harper and Row, 1966. [also: Canadian edition: 1st (1973) to 9th (1997)]

Lipton, Charles. *The Trade Union Movement of Canada, 1827–1959*. Montreal: Canadian Social Publications, 1966 [i.e., 1967].

Little, Jean. *From Anna*. Illustrated by Joan Sandin. New York: Harper and Row, 1972.

Lunn, Janet, and Christopher Moore. *The Story of Canada*. Illustrated by Alan Daniel. Toronto: Lester Publishing/Key Porter Books, 1992.

McClelland, Jack. *Imagining Canadian Literature: The Selected Letters of Jack McClelland*. Edited by Sam Solecki. Toronto: Key Porter, 1998.

McClung, Nellie L. *Clearing in the West: My Own Story*. Toronto: Thomas Allen, 1935.

MacDonald, Ann-Marie. *Fall on Your Knees*. Toronto: Alfred A. Knopf Canada, 1996.

MacEwen, Gwendolyn. *The Shadow-Maker*. Toronto: Macmillan of Canada, 1969.

MacLennan, Hugh. *Two Solitudes*. Toronto: Collins, 1945.

McLuhan, Marshall, and Quentin Fiore. *The Medium Is the Massage*. Co-ordinated by Jerome Agel. New York, Toronto: Bantam Books, 1967.

Maillet, Antonine. *Pélagie*. Translated by Philip Stratford. Toronto: General Publishing, 1982.

Maillet, Antonine. *Pélagie-la-Charrette: roman*. Montréal: Leméac, 1979.

Major, Kevin. *Hold Fast*. Toronto: Clarke, Irwin, 1978.

Mellen, Peter. *The Group of Seven*. Toronto: McClelland and Stewart, 1970.

Michaels, Anne. *Fugitive Pieces*. Toronto: McClelland and Stewart, 1996.

Miner, Jack. *Jack Miner and the Birds, and Some Things I Know about Nature*. Toronto: The Ryerson Press, 1923

Mintzberg, Henry. *The Nature of Managerial Work*. New York: Harper and Row, 1973.

Mistry, Rohinton. *A Fine Balance*. Toronto: McClelland and Stewart, 1995.

Mitchell, W. O. *Who Has Seen the Wind*. Toronto: Macmillan of Canada, 1947.

Montgomery, Lucy Maud. *Anne of Green Gables*. Boston: L. C. Page and Company, 1908.

Mowat, Farley. *Owls in the Family*. Illustrated by Robert Frankenberg. Boston: Little, Brown, 1961.

Mowat, Farley. *Sea of Slaughter*. Illustrated by Rob Tuckerman. Toronto: McClelland and Stewart, 1984.

Munro, Alice. *Lives of Girls and Women: A Novel*. Toronto, New York: McGraw-Hill Ryerson, 1971.

Munsch, Robert. *The Paper Bag Princess*. Illustrated by Michael Martchenko. Munsch for Kids. Toronto: Annick Press, 1980.

National Film Board of Canada. *Canada: A Year of the Land*. Lorraine Monk, executive producer; Bruce Hutchison, text; Allan Fleming, design. Centennial edition to mark the 100th anniversary of the Confederation of Canada. [Catalogue No. SP 72–1] [Ottawa]: Queen's Printer, 1967.

Newman, Peter C. *The Acquisitors*. Canadian Establishment, vol. 2. Toronto: McClelland and Stewart, 1981.

Newman, Peter C. *The Canadian Establishment*. Canadian Establishment, vol. 1. Toronto: McClelland and Stewart, 1975.

Newman, Peter C. *Titans: How the New Canadian Establishment Seized Power*. Canadian Establishment, vol. 3. Toronto: Viking, 1998.

Nostbakken, Janis, and Jack Humphrey. *The Canadian Inventions Book: Innovations, Discoveries, and Firsts*. Toronto: Greey de Pencier Publications, 1976.

Ondaatje, Michael. *The Collected Works of Billy the Kid: Left Handed Poems*. Toronto: Anansi, 1970.

Ondaatje, Michael. *The English Patient: A Novel*. Toronto: McClelland and Stewart, 1992.

Pearson, Kit. *The Guests of War Trilogy*. Toronto: Puffin, 1998.

Pearson, Kit. *Looking at the Moon*. Toronto: Viking, 1991.

Pearson, Kit. *The Lights Go on Again*. Toronto: Viking, 1993.

Pearson, Kit. *The Sky Is Falling*. Markham, Ont.: Viking Kestrel, 1989.

Porter, John. *The Vertical Mosaic: An Analysis of Social Class and Power in Canada*. Studies in the Structure of Power. Decision-Making in Canada, no. 2. Toronto: University of Toronto Press, 1965.

Priest, Lisa. *Conspiracy of Silence*. Toronto: McClelland and Stewart, 1989.

Purdy, Al. *The Collected Poems of Al Purdy*. Russell Brown, ed. Toronto: McClelland and Stewart, 1986.

Richler, Mordecai. *The Apprenticeship of Duddy Kravitz*. Don Mills, Ont.; London: André Deutsch, 1959.

Richler, Mordecai. *Jacob Two-Two Meets the Hooded Fang*. Illustrated by Fritz Wegner. Toronto: McClelland and Stewart, 1975.

Ross, Sinclair. *As For Me and My House: A Novel*. New York: Reynal and Hitchcock, 1941.

Roy, Gabrielle. *La petite poule d'eau*. [Montréal]: Éditions Beauchemin, 1950.

Roy, Gabrielle. *Where Nests the Water Hen: A Novel*. Translated by Harry L. Binsse. 1st ed. New York: Harcourt, Brace, 1951.

Royal Canadian Air Force. *5BX [i.e. Five Basic Exercises] Plan for Physical Fitness*. RCAF pamphlet, 30/1. Ottawa: Queen's Printer, 1958.

Rybczynski, Witold. *Home: A Short History of an Idea*. New York: Viking, 1986.

Ryga, George. *The Ecstasy of Rita Joe*. Vancouver: Talonplays, 1970.

Scott, Jay. *Great Scott!: The Best of Jay Scott's Movie Reviews*. Karen York, ed. [Introduction by Robert Fulford.] Toronto: McClelland and Stewart, 1994.

Selye, Hans. *The Stress of Life*. New York: McGraw-Hill, McGraw-Hill Paperbacks, 1956.

Service, Robert. *The Best of Robert Service*. Toronto: McGraw-Hill Ryerson, 1953.

Seton, Ernest Thompson. *Life-Histories of Northern Animals: An Account of the Mammals of Manitoba*. 2 vols. New York: C. Scribner's Sons, 1909.

Shields, Carol. *The Stone Diaries*. Toronto: Random House of Canada, 1993.

Smart, Elizabeth. *By Grand Central Station I Sat Down and Wept*. London: Editions Poetry London, 1945.

Smart, Tom. *The Art of Mary Pratt: Substance of Light*. [Fredericton, N.B.]: Goose Lane Editions, Beaverbrook Art Gallery, 1995.

Stewart, Hilary. *Cedar: Tree of Life to the Northwest Coast Indians*. Vancouver, Toronto: Douglas and McIntyre; Seattle: University of Washington Press, 1984.

Strong-Boag, Veronica, and Anita Clair Fellman, eds. *Rethinking Canada: The Promise of Women's History*. New Canadian Readings. Toronto: Copp Clark Pitman, 1986. Also: 2nd ed., 1991; 3rd ed., 1997.

Town, Harold, and David Silcox. *Tom Thomson: The Silence and the Storm*. Toronto: McClelland and Stewart, 1977.

Tremblay, Michel. *Les Belles Soeurs*. Translated by John Van Burek and Bill Glassco. Vancouver: Talonbooks, 1974.

Tremblay, Michel. *Les belles-soeurs*. Théâtre vivant. Montréal: Holt, Rinehart et Winston, 1968.

Walker, George F. *Zastrozzi, The Master of Discipline: A Melodrama*. Toronto: Playwrights Co-op, 1977.

Watson, Sheila. *The Double Hook*. Toronto: McClelland and Stewart, 1959.

Weisbord, Merrily, and Merilyn Simonds Mohr. *The Valour and the Horror: The Untold Story of Canadians in the Second World War*. Toronto: HarperCollins, 1991.

Wilson, Ethel. *Swamp Angel*. Toronto: Macmillan, 1954.

Wyman, Max. *Dance Canada: An Illustrated History*. Vancouver, Toronto: Douglas and McIntyre, 1989.

Wynne-Jones, Tim. *The Maestro: A Novel*. Vancouver, Toronto: Douglas and McIntyre, Groundwood Books, 1995.

Yee, Paul. *Tales from Gold Mountain: Stories of the Chinese in the New World*. Illustrated by Simon Ng. Vancouver, Toronto: Douglas and McIntyre, Groundwood Books, 1989.

Index of Titles

Index of Authors, Editors, Illustrators and Translators